New Studies in the Philosophy of Religion

General Editor: W. D. Hudson, Reader in Moral Philosophy,
University of Exeter

This series of monographs includes studies of all the main
problems in the philosophy of religion. It will be of particular
interest to those who study this subject in universities or colleges.
The philosophical problems connected with religious belief are
not, however, a subject of concern only to specialists; they arise
in one form or another for all intelligent men when confronted
by the appeals or the claims of religion.

The general approach of this series is from the standpoint of
contemporary analytical philosophy, and the monographs are
written by a distinguished team of philosophers, all of whom
now teach, or have recently taught, in British or American
universities. Each author has been commissioned to analyse
some aspect of religious belief; to set forth clearly and concisely
the philosophical problems which arise from it; to take into
account the solutions which classical or contemporary philosophers have offered; and to present his own critical assessment
of how religious belief now stands in the light of these problems
and their proposed solutions.

In the main it is theism with which these monographs deal,
because that is the type of religious belief with which readers
are most likely to be familiar, but other forms of religion are not
ignored. Some of the authors are religious believers and some
are not, but it is not their primary aim to write polemically,
much less dogmatically, for or against religion. Rather, they
set themselves to clarify the nature of religious belief in the light
of modern philosophy by bringing into focus the questions about
it which a reasonable man as such has to ask. How is talk of
God like, and how unlike, other universes of discourse in which
men engage, such as science, art or morality? Is this talk of
God self-consistent? Does it accord with other rational beliefs
which we hold about man or the world which he inhabits? It
is questions such as these which this series will help the reader
to answer for himself.

New Studies in the Philosophy of Religion

IN THE SAME SERIES

Published

In preparation

Scepticism

KAI NIELSEN
The University of Calgary

Macmillan
St. Martin's Press

First published 1973 by
THE MACMILLAN PRESS LTD
London and Basingstoke
Associated companies in New York Toronto
Dublin Melbourne Johannesburg and Madras

Library of Congress catalog card no. 72-77776

SBN 333 10263 0

Printed in Great Britain by
R & R CLARK LTD
Edinburgh

To my parents

Contents

General Editor's Preface

In this important monograph Professor Nielsen has presented a defence of scepticism which is thoroughly up to date. He is fully acquainted with contemporary work on the philosophy of religion and his study takes account of the latest moves in Christian apologetics. Whether or not the reader is disposed to share the author's sceptical conclusions, this monograph will be of the greatest interest to all who consider that religious belief is a matter about which intelligent men must make up their minds. Students of philosophy will find it particularly valuable as stating, with admirable clarity and vigour, one influential point of view in the contemporary debate about religion.

University of Exeter   W. D. HUDSON

Acknowledgements

I have been helped in various ways in the writing of this essay. Professor Adel Daher and Rodger Beehler have made useful criticisms of an earlier draft of the manuscript and fruitful discussions with George Monticone have led to some changes in what I say about verificationism. Kurt Neureither and Gary Kodish painstakingly read the proofs. My wife, Elisabeth Nielsen, has also both perceptively criticised the manuscript and uncomplainingly borne up under the burden of proofreading. Finally, Beverly Forbes and Rhoda Blythe have conscientiously, accurately and speedily typed the manuscript. I am grateful indeed for this varied assistance. My blunders, of course, remain my own (to make a 'grammatical remark' with a point).

KAI NIELSEN

The University of Calgary
September 1972

1 Varieties of Scepticism

Philosophical scepticism has few defenders nowadays. It has several forms but only in one very attenuated form has it had anything coming close to a convincing defence. A Pyrrhonian sceptic, for example, claims that we never have good grounds for adopting a definite position on anything because for every argument in favour of a particular doctrine or claim there is an equally strong argument against this argument or claim. This Pyrrhonian scepticism is distinct from two key forms of modern scepticism, namely (1) the form which claims that we know nothing, i.e. that nobody knows anything about anything, and (2) that we only know the contents of our own minds. If the Pyrrhonian sceptic is claiming to know the truth of the generalisation that for every argument in support of a doctrine or claim there is an equally strong argument against it, he is asserting something which is actually incompatible with those modern forms of scepticism because the Pyrrhonian, in claiming the above, is claiming much more than they claim and indeed is claiming something that could not be justifiably claimed if either of these modern forms of scepticism were true. However, the Pyrrhonian could readily weaken his claim to the claim that he reasonably believes this to be so or that he just finds it to be the case. But such claims are plainly absurd. It is surely not the case that for every argument the arguments pro and con utterly balance out. Something might be said for the arguments of flat earthers, but it could hardly be reasonably claimed that their arguments are as plausible as the arguments of their opponents. Pyrrhonism only attains a *semblance* of plausibility if it is altered to the quite different thesis that there is no rational resolution of an argument which is so utterly decisive that we can be *certain* that the truth has been established concerning the disputed claims.

1

If to know P entails being certain of P, then this *altered* statement of Pyrrhonism reduces to the first modern form of scepticism characterised above. That is to say, it reduces to the claim that nobody knows anything about anything. But this is not traditionally what Pyrrhonism has been about. However, in any of its traditional forms Pyrrhonism presents no serious philosophical challenge at all.

The modern forms of scepticism also have few takers. The arguments of Moore, Wittgenstein, Ayer, Chisholm and Strawson against such scepticism have created a philosophical climate in which philosophical scepticism is not taken seriously. At best it is thought of as a purely formal challenge designed to query whether we can give an utterly airtight account of our common sense and scientific knowledge, but there is no real doubt at all concerning whether we know that there are tables and chairs or whether we know that the earth goes around the sun. What survives, as a reasonably serious philosophical contender, is the claim that we human beings at best know hardly anything to be so.[1] But the defender of this claim – itself a very controversial claim – remarks that he happily accepts 'the fact that there is much that many of us correctly and reasonably believe. . . .'[2]

The situation is very different for religious scepticism. Unlike philosophical scepticism, religious scepticism is not thought to be a paradoxical philosophical thesis – a purely academic exercise – but is thought by many intellectuals to be a commonplace and is pervasively accepted by large numbers of educated people and indeed by many uneducated people as well. Here the doubts are not Cartesian doubts but doubts Peirce characterised as 'real doubts'.[3]

Religious scepticism has been grounded in philosophical scepticism, but so has fideism. But what is important to see in this context is that contemporary religious scepticism is typically not at all grounded in philosophical scepticism. The arguments developed here for religious scepticism will not turn on the acceptance of philosophical scepticism in any of its forms, and certain fideistic responses to religious scepticism do not gain much plausibility by an appeal to such a dubious construction as philosophical scepticism. Moreover, we should not forget the point stressed by both Hume and Russell, that even if philosophical scepticism can be stated in a logically impeccable manner, there is an evident frivolous insincerity in any attempt to accept it and act in accordance with it. Philosophical scepticism, they argued, can only be taken seriously as a doctrine concerned with the *grounds* for our knowledge claims; it is not something that can be lived or genuinely believed. That is to say, we can have Cartesian methodological doubts but not real doubts. But this is not so for religious doubts. With those doubts the engine is not idling, for they often deeply affect our lives. Some come to reject a religious orientation altogether because of such considerations, others become indifferent to the whole question of religious faith and still others come to adopt forms of fideism in which they are either tortured with doubt or come to hold their religious beliefs in a markedly different way as a result of the influence of scepticism concerning religion.

Indeed, there are people with a philosophical turn of mind who have doubts about religious scepticism: they doubt in a methodological manner whether in this domain there is really anything to doubt. But this does not lead them to believe that religious beliefs are true or lead them to any acceptance of them.

II

There are four additional preliminary points that should be borne in mind in considering scepticism concerning religion.

First, the distinction in this domain between believers and sceptics has a certain elasticity to it. In the dialectic of the argument between belief and unbelief, often what is taken in some quarters as belief will be regarded in other quarters as unbelief, idolatry or gross superstition indicating a lack of 'true belief', and what is taken by some to be a kind of intellectually chastened fideism will appear to others as a form of scepticism. It is by no means easy to say what counts as 'true religion', 'the essence of religion' or 'the essence of Christianity'. It is indeed true that with such talk *persuasive* definitions are at work and normative questions get raised, but it doesn't follow from this that one answer is as good as another and that we can only commit ourselves one way or another or that there are not key troubling issues here which require philosophical assessment.

Secondly, in talking about religious belief, I shall have in mind primarily Christian belief. But what I shall say for the most part applies also to Jewish and Moslem beliefs. I do not

3

at all suggest that these sister beliefs are superior to Hindu, Buddhist or Confucian religious beliefs. I do not for a minute believe that that is true. But Christianity is by far the most pervasive religious belief in our culture and provides for most people, within our environment, the sole serious religious option. In our culture, it is for most people either Christianity or a secular outlook. There are some conversions to Judaism or Islam but they are infrequent. However, in considering scepticism about religion, I shall be concerned for the most part with scepticism about those central doctrines of Christianity which are also assented to by Jews and Moslems. It is these doctrines and arguments supportive of them that we shall query sceptically.

Thirdly, in contrasting religious scepticism and philosophical scepticism, I meant by 'religious scepticism' general philosophical scepticism concerning religion (primarily central strands of Christian belief). There is a sense of 'religious scepticism' in which one, as was the case with Pascal, Hamann and Kierkegaard, can be both sceptical and religious. It is even sometimes maintained that 'truly religious' people – as with some of Dostoyevsky's characters – must be religious sceptics. And more cautiously, Ninian Smart reminds us that 'saintliness and doubts often go together'.[4] But as I use 'religious sceptic', a fideist cannot be a religious sceptic. In speaking of a 'religious sceptic' I am speaking of either an atheist or an agnostic. By an 'atheist' I shall mean someone who rejects belief in God because he believes that it is false or probably false that such a reality exists, or because he believes that the concept of God is so incoherent or problematical that one cannot intelligibly or justifiably assert that it is either true or false that there is such a reality or, lastly, because he believes that the word 'God' really *only* stands for or is only expressive of a purely secular reality. A man is an agnostic if he has a tendency to believe what the atheist believes but also has a tendency to believe the opposite as well and cannot decide what is most reasonable to believe in this domain and indeed believes either that there can be no rational resolution to this question or that it is unlikely that there will be such a resolution.

Fourthly, and finally, as should be evident from the above, there are varieties of religious scepticism, or, as I shall henceforth call it, 'scepticism', and arguments supportive of one form

4

will not necessarily support another, and to find the most important form or forms of scepticism is also to discover what is central to a defence of religious faith.

A religious sceptic, as I use the term, is an atheist or agnostic. And my specification of the sense of these terms specifies what I intend by 'religious scepticism'. But what I need to do now is to spell out somewhat more fully what is involved in such scepticism. What we want to know, be we sceptics or believers, is can we know that God exists (that there is an X such that X is God) or reasonably believe that God exists or justifiably believe that God exists or even make any sense of that notion at all so that we could intelligibly believe or even fail to believe in God. A sceptic either doubts or positively rejects the contention that we can know or rightly believe any or all of these things. There are theologians such as Ninian Smart and I. T. Ramsey who believe they can establish the truth of the claim that 'it is reasonable to believe in the truth of Christianity'. A sceptic must doubt this and indeed doubt this for any belief in supernatural or transcendent realities. He must not believe that we can know or reasonably believe or indeed justifiably accept as articles of faith 'that the physical universe owes its existence to an immaterial personal being, that the death of Jesus Christ on the cross constituted an atonement for the sins of men, and that the Bible is the word of God'.[5] He must believe that it is not the case that we can give reasonable grounds for believing in these central doctrines of Christianity. There are fideists who also believe that we cannot give reasonable grounds for believing that the doctrines of Christianity are true but continue to believe in them all the same. The religious sceptic, by contrast, can neither believe that they are true nor believe in them – accept them on faith.

It is important to keep in mind that religious scepticism need not be, as many Christian theologians aver that it is, a matter of a sinful turning away from God by a man whose heart has been hardened or sense of morality dulled; rather it can be, and characteristically is, as Ninian Smart well puts it, a rejection of religion 'because they find Christianity unpersuasive, incredible.

5

It is not that they do not *want* to believe it: it is just that they *cannot* believe it.'[6]

The inability to believe comes from two principal sources: (1) from a conviction that there is no evidence or far too little evidence for such beliefs, (2) from a conviction that the evidence against such beliefs is so considerable as to make it unreasonable to believe them, and (3) from a conviction that God-talk just does not make sense, i.e. that it is incomprehensible, incoherent, unintelligible or meaningless. It had been repeatedly asserted that a characteristic difference between contemporary scepticism, influenced heavily by positivism, and earlier forms of scepticism, is that the latter doubted that we could know whether the central Christian claims concerning God are *true*, while the former doubts that fundamental Christian claims concerning God have any cognitive meaning. This, I believe, is oversimplified and not altogether historically accurate. Questions of meaning and truth tend in certain contexts to get run together and not without reason. But surely later scepticism is more self-consciously concerned with questions of meaning and it is at least pedagogically useful to keep these questions apart. Where what is thought to be at issue are the more traditional sceptical questions concerning truth-finding, the central sceptical questions concerning Christian and generally theistic doctrines are:

(1) Can we know that these doctrines are true?
(2) Can we reasonably believe that these doctrines are true?
(3) Can we reasonably remain or become Christians even though we have no *adequate* grounds for believing that these doctrines are true?
(4) Can we reasonably remain or become Christians even though we have *no grounds at all* for believing that these doctrines are true?

With the possible exception of (4), sceptics, contemporary or otherwise, must answer these questions in the negative, though their grounds for giving negative answers may differ. In addition, a characteristically contemporary form of scepticism, concerned very much with questions of meaning, will ask the following questions or a cluster of questions bearing a close family resemblance to them:

(5) Can we know or reasonably believe that there is a viable

6

concept of God which is sufficiently intelligible or coherent such that Christian belief could be (a) justifiable,
or (b) believable, or (c) even intelligible?
(6) Can we know or reasonably believe that the central
putative truth-claims of Christianity are genuine truth-
claims, i.e. make statements which are true or false?

A sceptic could answer (5) or (6) either in part or in whole
affirmatively and still remain a sceptic, but a characteristically
contemporary form of scepticism tends to answer (5) or (6),
either in part or in whole, negatively. The feeling is – to put it
crudely and collapsing several distinct considerations into one –
the central claims of Christianity, the core bits of God-talk, do
not make sense.

I will start by asking if they do. And indeed, I shall concentrate most centrally on sceptical questions of this type. That
is, I will begin with and continue (for the most part) to concentrate on these logically prior questions, for if the sceptic's
case is a good one here, there is no need even to consider
questions (1) through (4), for then they do not even arise. For
example, if the key religious utterances can be neither true nor
false, then they clearly cannot be true and there is no point at all
in asking if we can know or reasonably believe that they are
true. And if there is nothing that can be intelligibly believed,
then there is no possibility of taking something on faith without
evidence or without grounds or even in spite of the evidence,
for we would not be able to understand *what* we are to take on
faith and thus an act of faith would not be possible. In *that
sense*, understanding must precede faith.[7]

With this ambiguity cleared away, let us return to our consideration of the rationale behind scepticism concerning the
intelligibility of God-talk. However, before I go on to consider
one of the foremost reasons for believing that religious claims
do not make sense, I need to clear up an ambiguity embedded
in some of the above questions, namely, how are we to take
'reasonably believe'? There is a reading in which it is perfectly
evident that people do reasonably believe that these doctrines
are intelligible and indeed true. It is a reading in which 'reasonably believe' refers *to the way in which the holder holds his views*.
He does not 'reasonably believe' if his mind is closed to opposite
views, if he is intolerant of the beliefs and convictions of others,

7

if he deliberately refuses to consider arguments or putative evidence against his beliefs, if he stubbornly refuses even to consider the possibility that he might be mistaken and the like.[8] If he eschews such a way of holding beliefs and overcomes evident forms of ignorance and bias and is genuinely open-minded and attuned to the core considerations, given his situation in life and the information available to him, we can correctly say that he 'reasonably believes'.

On such a reading, it is evident enough that, even among the intelligentsia, there are plenty of Christians who reasonably believe that their God-talk is intelligible and reasonably believe that their religious doctrines are true. However, in asking the above questions, I intended a different reading of 'reasonably believe' in which the correct answer is not so easily settled. Here, I am directing a question at the belief itself. In asking the question, I am asking it as an agent would ask a question of his *own beliefs*. For me to allow it to be the case that I reasonably believe P, I must allow it to be the case that I have good reasons to believe P to be true or I must have good reasons for believing that there are others – reasonable and informed people – in a good position to know about P who believe P to be true. So in asking about 'reasonably believe' in (2), I am asking whether there are good reasons for believing that those doctrines are true and in (6), I am asking whether there are good reasons for believing those putative truth-claims are genuine truth-claims.

One of the grounds often given for the belief that religious claims do not make sense is that they are not verifiable and/or falsifiable. Religious claims purport to be true, but truth requires evidence or grounds; that is, we can never know a claim to be true unless we have evidence or grounds for that claim. So if the central claims of our God-talk are indeed true, if they correctly make fundamental assertions about what is the case, they must at least be verifiable or falsifiable. But God-talk is either like Zeus-talk, in that it is anthropomorphic and makes straightforwardly false claims, or, unlike Zeus-talk, it is non-anthropomorphic and makes putative truth-claims which are neither verifiable nor falsifiable even in principle and, hence, are in reality not genuine truth-claims.

In my *Contemporary Critiques of Religion*, I have examined this falsification challenge at some length and have argued that a carefully qualified and more precise statement of it does have

8

considerable sceptical force. I neither want to repeat that argument here nor make my present arguments depend on what I argued there. To bring the central considerations concerning such a form of scepticism to the fore here, I shall, in the remainder of this chapter, set out two model arguments which attempt, in very distinct ways, to meet *this* sceptical argument. I shall attempt to show how they fail and in doing so bring out something of the force of this argument. I shall then proceed in Chapter Two to examine an important and sophisticated attempt to make sense of religion which utterly by-passes such considerations and indeed metaphysical considerations altogether. I shall try to show that such an approach cannot justifiably obviate such difficulties or rightly quiet sceptical doubts. I then turn in Chapter Three to an examination of an approach to religion which attempts to work empirically (from the facts of religious experience) to show that such sceptical arguments are misdirected. I shall try to show here that it is precisely when we carefully examine such claims from religious experience that we come to see how questions of the intelligibility of God-talk arise in full force. In Chapter Four I try to exhibit the full force of the sceptical challenge concerning the intelligibility of God-talk by critically examining the quite varied attempts of some distinguished theologians to meet it, and finally, in Chapter Five, I return again to the core sceptical considerations of the present chapter and attempt in sum to show why we should be sceptics.

IV

The first model argument (exemplified in the work of John Wilson and Hugo Meynell) attempts to meet this falsification challenge head-on by establishing that certain key religious claims are plainly falsifiable.[9] Meynell, for example, maintains this to be so not only for anthropomorphic God-talk but also for what he regards as traditional theism in its sophisticated non-anthropomorphic formulations. His arguments are typical of a certain quite natural response to such a challenge and are, in part, directed to meeting some earlier sceptical arguments of mine. In articulating my first model argument, I shall follow out his central contentions.

Meynell thinks that it is 'perfectly easy to show what it is for it to be true, what it is for it to be false' to assert 'God created man in His image and likeness' or 'In God alone is man sustained'. By contrast, the kind of scepticism we are presently considering maintains that such claims are only *putatively* factual. Traditional theists want certain of their key claims to have truth-value – to be central assertions of cosmological fact – but the sceptic's claim is that their very use of 'God' in such sentences is such that when we try to employ them to make assertions what is said in reality has no truth-value. If a proposition P is alleged to have truth-value but we can never find out what its truth-value is, then we (1), are justified, to a minimal extent, in claiming that it is without value as a truth-claim and (2), and somewhat more controversially, we have good reasons for being sceptical as to whether this alleged truth-claim is indeed a genuine truth-claim.

Meynell is undisturbed by such claims, for he believes that what counts for or against the truth of such religious propositions can readily be shown. In examining his arguments, it is crucial to see that we are trying to ascertain whether non-anthropomorphic and non-reductionist religious claims succeed in making intelligible truth-claims whose truth-value we can indeed ascertain.[10]

Before we proceed further, I should make clear what I mean by 'an anthropomorphic conception of God' and 'a non-anthropomorphic conception of God'. If God is conceived in anthropomorphic terms, He is, in important respects, Zeus-like. That is to say, on such a conception of God it is an open question whether God could be literally seen or heard; such a God is so person-like that we could literally conceive of His speaking to us or to others, of our meeting Him and the like. Such a God is indeed a determinate being among beings, though indeed a being of most extraordinary characteristics. With such a conception of God, putatively assertive God-talk is quite verifiable, but what is said, as both Meynell and I and almost everyone else agree, is for the most part just plainly false. Non-anthropomorphic conceptions of God, by contrast, are largely characterisable as a denial of the claims of anthropomorphic theism. God, given such a conception, is not a being among beings; any being, as Ninian Smart and Frederick Copleston stress, which could literally be seen or encountered would by definition not be God.[11] There is no identifying God as one

10

might identify an object or process. To think that God could be so identified is to fail to understand what is meant by 'God' in developed Christian and Jewish streams of life. God is not even an extraordinary being in the domain of beings, but is, on the non-anthropomorphic conception of God which coincides with 'sophisticated traditional theism', Being itself, an utterly infinite, unlimited, eternal, self-existent reality, transcendent to the world and upon whom all finite realities in the world depend, though this infinite, utterly independent, ultimate reality does not depend on anything else itself either for its existence or value. When we add that this 'ultimate reality' is supremely worthy of worship, we have the core conception of what Meynell calls 'sophisticated traditional theism'.

I agree with Meynell that such a conception of God is at the heart of classical Judaism and Christianity, but, as this essay will try to show, there are good reasons for believing that such a conception of God is so incoherent that it is something we cannot intelligibly believe in. My contention shall be that given such a conception of God, 'God created man in his image and likeness', 'In God alone man is sustained' and indeed even 'God exists' are all so problematic as to be devoid of any genuine truth-value.

Let us label 'God created man in his image and likeness', as (1) and try to ascertain whether (1) is a genuine factual truth-claim, i.e. whether (1) is even weakly confirmable or infirmable. Meynell believes there are events in nature and history which show what it would be like for this putative statement to be true and that we also can conceive of events which count against its truth. If things have turned out, are turning out, and will turn out in a certain way, then (1), Meynell avers, is true. If things did not turn out and are not turning out in this way, then we would have good reason to think (1) false. The particular states of affairs in the past that count for the truth of (1) are, as Meynell puts it, 'the life, death and resurrection of Jesus Christ . . .'

We must, however, be careful here just how we talk, for if, as Hepburn points out in *Christianity and Paradox*, we invoke the notion of Christ, we invoke the notion of the son of God and we are back to the very problematical concept of God whose coherence is in question. We must be more circumspect and stick with Jesus – a being plainly identifiable and a being whose actions were quite identifiable. That is to say, there are here

11

particular, determinate states of affairs the existence of which can be quite readily ascertained. For similar reasons, we should fight shy of talking about the resurrection, for this notion seems at least to involve the notion of disembodied existence – a notion which is itself, to put it mildly, of problematical intelligibility.[12]

Because of these considerations, let us stick with that part of Jesus' life and activity that can be characterised in terms which plainly do have truth-value. What then, if anything, in His life and death tends to show (1) to be true? Let us take at face value the claim that Jesus so loved human beings that He was prepared to die for them. He, let us agree, showed love and compassion for men in a superlative degree. But atheists such as Santayana and Feuerbach were perfectly aware of such considerations and yet this did not incline them to believe. They could have even come to agree that this characterisation correctly characterised Jesus and yet have remained atheists. Were they just stubbornly flying in the face of the evidence or in some double-minded manner (to use Kierkegaard's conception) rationalising? With thinkers of such profound religious sensibilities and knowledge, it is difficult to believe that this is so. And after all, why should the fact that a man existed, who was extraordinary in compassion and love, tend *at all* to show that there exists an infinite, eternal, self-existent individual transcendent to the world? A man from Mars or from a strange tribe who had never heard God-talk or talk of realities transcendent to the world could come to understand perfectly well what is meant by such talk of love and compassion and still remain utterly perplexed about what was meant by 'infinite individual', 'transcendent to the world', 'self-existent being' and the like. He could find these notions utterly opaque and thus the traditional non-anthropomorphic conception of God opaque, and yet still understand the purely secular and comparatively unproblematical talk of love and compassion. He wants to know *what* is this God we are talking about and why is the fact of such behaviour on the part of a human being (in this case, Jesus) *any evidence at all* that there is such a reality? Indeed, at an even more fundamental level, it would be natural for him to ask, 'Why believe that it would even enable us to understand what we are talking about when we use "God"?' Meynell does nothing at all to answer these questions, but until

12

and unless he or someone else can, the burden of proof is on such a theist to show that such behaviour on Jesus' part is a partial confirmation of (1), i.e. of 'God created man in his image and likeness'.

My point here may be misunderstood. The sceptic need not and indeed should not be asking for decisive confirmation or disconfirmation. This would indeed be absurd, for it would require of God-talk what we do not require of much of scientific discourse and indeed of other discourse as well whose coherence and intelligibility is firmly established. It is true that such a sceptic is given to understand that talk about Jesus' compassion and love and the like is equally compatible with a secular humanist and a Christian conceptual framework, but he is not only saying that. He is also asserting that no reason has been given to believe that such human behaviour is evidence for the truth of such putative statements as (1) and that such talk does not give 'God' any empirical or experiential anchorage so that we can come to understand what is being talked about.

Can anything in the present confirm or disconfirm to any degree at all (1) or, more generally, claims concerning the reality or providential care of God? As confirming evidence for such putative claims, Meynell offers the believer's experience of God's graciousness in his own life. To make this non-question-begging, we need some independent and purely empirical specification of the particular states of affairs covered by 'God's graciousness in his own life'.[13] But we need to understand in a quite literal way what is being talked about before we can ascertain what, if any, evidential weight such a putative claim has. But on this score, Meynell is not very helpful. He speaks of the believer's present experience of God through his private devotion and in the fellowship of the Church. Yet, if we have trouble with 'experience of God's graciousness', we will have similar trouble with the above phrase. If 'experience' has any clear meaning at all, it is a determinable for the more determinate notions of seeing, hearing, smelling, tasting, feeling and the like. But, as we have seen, a non-anthropomorphic God could not (logically) be seen, heard, felt, smelled, tasted and the like. And it is because of this that we should recognise that God could not reveal Himself to us or disclose Himself to us, for to do that God would have to be seeable, hearable, etc., but none of these things are logically possible where we are concerned with a non-anthropomorphic God. (This is no limitation of God's omnipotence because to be omnipotent one only needs to be able to do anything that it is logically possible to do.) We should also recognise that it does not help to talk of being aware of God, encountering God or meeting God, for all of these terms have the key difficulties that 'experience' has when used in that linguistic environment. Because of these crucial incoherencies in the very 'statements' taken to be evidential statements for 'The order in the world reflects God's providential care' and 'God created man in His image and likeness', we can hardly rightly claim to have statements which can be verified or falsified. We have not shown for these 'religious statements' that we understand what it would be like for them to be true or false.

Does anything in the future serve any better as confirmatory evidence for (1) or any other 'God-statement' of similar magnitude? Meynell speaks as if the truth of the following three statements would so serve: 'The unhappy will in the future be made happy', 'The oppressed will be made free', and 'Those who have striven for virtue will be rewarded'. There are religious thinkers who think poorly of the religious propriety of these remarks and I share this opinion; but here this is not to the point. They are intelligible enough and we have some idea of what would confirm them. But, again, an utter atheist or secularist could assert them. Indeed, many a good Marxist, utterly atheistic in his orientation to the world, strives to make it the case that the oppressed will be free and if he is reasonably orthodox, he will also believe that some day this will quite definitely be the case. In short, here we are in the same predicament we were in, in talking of Jesus' love and compassion. We are characterising discrete, empirically ascertainable particular states of affairs. But there is no good reason to believe that statements confirming that such states of affairs obtain do anything to confirm 'God created man in his image and likeness' or 'There is a God-given Providential ordering of the universe'. Note that if that latter statement is read as being simply an umbrella statement covering rather generally statements such as 'The oppressed will be made free', we actually have the kind of reductionist analysis that Meynell rejects. Presumably it asserts more, but we are left in the dark how to ascertain *what more* or how 'The oppressed will be made free' *confirms to the*

14

slightest degree transcendent religious claims (e.g. 'There is a God-given providential ordering of the universe').

Meynell makes an argument that might be construed as a counter to the line of argumentation I have taken here. He remarks there that it is to no avail to argue that 'even if Jesus acted just as the gospels say he did, and even if the ultimate fate of men turns out according to his promises – this still does not imply that a transcendent God exists'. It is to no avail because it leads such a sceptic, Meynell would have us believe, into making an arbitrary claim. That this is so, Meynell maintains, can be seen if we attend to a parallel remark to the remark quoted above. Suppose someone asserts 'Whatever movements are made by that body known as Jones, the mere fact of them does not make its direction by human intelligence logically necessary.' But if that body we call Jones reads, plays tennis, does trigonometry, recites poetry and the like, it would be arbitrary to deny that the movements of that body were directed by human intelligence. Similarly, Meynell contends, if the particular states of affairs we have talked about in talking about the confirmation of (1) were to obtain, it would be arbitrary to deny that God exists.

It would not, and when we see a crucial dis-analogy between the two allegedly parallel sentences, it will be evident why. Doing things like trigonometry, writing poetry, driving a car, reading and playing tennis are just the kinds of things we mean to refer to when we speak of 'intelligent or purposive behaviour'. 'Beethoven composed the Ninth Symphony but that was mere bodily movements exhibiting no intentional action' is at least close to incoherency. Similarly, we do not need to be logical behaviourists to realise that it just – as we use language – makes no sense at all to ascribe many such purposeful actions to the behaviour of Jones and deny that he is a creature with intelligence. But we can say without the slightest deviation from linguistic regularities or without any suggestion of conceptual incoherence that even if there is no God, the oppressed some day shall be free and the burden of human suffering shall be less. That statement may be false and wildly utopian, but it is not self-contradictory, in any way logically odd or conceptually out of order. Similar things should be said for the other straight-forwardly empirical statements we have culled from Meynell's several arguments that we know perfectly well what counts as

15

evidence for the truth of fundamental strands of God-talk. In this crucial respect Meynell's argument by analogy fails and thus his argument against the sceptic collapses.

The core consideration in this first model argument turned on what, if anything, actually can correctly be taken as counting as evidence for or against 'God created man in His image' and the like, where 'God' is constructed non-anthropomorphically and in traditional theistic terms. My argument has been that this is not nearly the unproblematic affair that theists such as Meynell and indeed even some atheists and agnostics take it to be. Meynell has not established that anything does or could so count so that we could have some understanding of whether the claims of non-anthropomorphic theism are either true or false.

The second model argument that I want to state and examine briefly takes such traditional Jewish and Christian theism as Meynell articulates to be an utter confusion and, in effect, idolatrous. It stresses that there is incoherence in the very concept of God as a transcendent being (an infinite individual) and sustaining transcendent cause distinct from the world and in no way dependent on the world.[14] If this is our view of God, it is maintained, then atheism is the only reasonable option. Such a God – that is, the God of 'sophisticated traditional theism' – could never have existed. There is, however, in contrast to theism another central strand of religious thought, including Jewish and Christian thought, which does not fall prey to the sceptical criticisms directed against traditional theism. It is important in this connection to recognise that there is a fairly clear distinction in every religion between the 'popular' and the 'esoteric', between the worship of the 'householder' and that of the monk. (We must not forget that what may be idolatry and/ or superstition to one man will be genuine religious belief to another.) It is not enough for the sceptical critic of religion to show, say with respect to Judaism or Christianity, that the popular conceptions of God are either incoherent or commit believers to plainly false beliefs. The critic must show that these considerations hold for the 'esoteric' conceptions of the monks as well.

Marcia Cavell, who argues in this way, articulates in a philosophically sophisticated way what she takes to be the core considerations embedded in these conceptions.[15] I want to probe

16

the coherence of her account. My contention will be that this second model argument, different as it is from our first model argument, suffers from similar conceptual difficulties concerning its ability to make intelligible truth-claims. Here the sceptical problem remains, if I am right, essentially the same.

In trying to give a perspicuous representation of a concept of God in which 'God' is neither a name nor a truncated description of an extraordinary personal being, Cavell attempts to give us readings of 'There is a God', 'God is within us' or 'I believe in God' which are coherent and religiously attractive, i.e. they would give a religiously sensitive and philosophically sophisticated person a conception of God which (a) would not be a scandal to the intellect and (b) would give him or her a conception of something which was worthy of worship. Cavell's claim is that such bits of God-talk are 'statements which acknowledge and commit one to a certain kind of relationship between one's self and the whole of one's world.' Taken by itself, this is simply a dark saying, and we need to see the elucidation that she gives it.

In looking for a clue as to how we are to read statements about God, Cavell points to what she takes to be the fact that our relations to God can never be contingent. This is so, she avers, because our interest in God is not just theoretical, for to 'say that I believe in God is always to assert that there is a relationship which I acknowledge between myself and something else'. But this very acknowledgement involves a commitment and thus something which is non-contingent. But if God is not a supernatural entity or a transcendent being or any kind of being at all, *what* is it that we stand in a relation to and *what* is the nature of that relationship? Cavell tells us that to talk about God is to talk about the world, i.e. man's relationship to his world, in a certain way. The proper reading for 'I believe in God' is 'I hold a certain attitude, which is religious, toward *everything* to which I am inescapably related; namely the world as I experience it'.

Here it is difficult for me to believe that Cavell means just what she says. For, if she does, then we would have to say that an atheist believed in God if he had attitudes toward the world (propositional attitudes apart) which were identical to those of Christians. (Think here of someone like Santayana.) But such conversion by stipulative re-definition is surely illegitimate.

17

It could be countered that Cavell is not talking about the plain man's beliefs but about the beliefs of the religiously sophisticated and that there, as Kierkegaard and Bultmann have stressed, the difference between a certain kind of religiously sensitive atheist and a religious believer is not at all clear. But this is not how these atheists see it and it is not how the vast majority of 'esoteric believers' see it themselves. While they realised that a Feuerbach, Eliot or Santayana might say penetrating and significant things about religion and have a genuine feel for religious ways of life, they did not believe that they believed in God, for to believe in God is *not only* to have a certain attitude toward that to which one is inescapably related, but it is also to think that it is true that there is a transcendent, wholly other reality. Cavell has confused a necessary condition for belief in God with a sufficient condition.[16]

It is probably false that Cavell's reading of 'believe in God' is even a characterisation of a central strand of Jewish or Christian belief, but let us, all the same, for the sake of the discussion, assume that it is *a correct* characterisation of what is involved in belief in God in some central strand of Judaism and/or Christianity. Even so, is it a helpful characterisation which enlightens us about belief in God? On the credit side, it does stress how commitment goes with religious belief and it does not, at least in any obvious way, involve any incoherent concepts in its characterisation of religious belief. But, crucially, on the debit side (or so it seems to me) it blurs any distinction between a religiously sensitive scepticism and religious belief. And this is a distinction we would want to keep to be clear about religious truth-claims and to be clear what kind of commitment goes with a religious way of life. Kierkegaard realised that to understand what religious belief is, it is sometimes well to go to the man who rejects religion. But he still did not confuse him with the believer. He recognised that there was a distinction between belief and unbelief, even though the believer could be beset by doubt and perplexity.

Moreover, even in the esoteric traditions of Christianity, there are evident difficulties in explaining the 'what' in 'What is this God that is being talked about, believed in or disbelieved in?' when 'God' is construed as referring to the world as the believer experiences it. And even if, following Kierkgaard, we stress the 'how' of belief and not the 'what', we still cannot in

18

the last analysis escape the question of *what* it is that we believe in when we believe in God. If what answers to the 'what' is an illusion, then no matter with what integrity one believes, one is still caught up in a myth, and indeed no 'saving myth' at that, for it is, as an illusion, something one is not justified in believing. And there are difficulties as well in trying to make religious sense of this talk, for, as Ninian Smart (to whom Cavell is indebted) remarks, even in esoteric traditions of Christianity such systems of salvation have integral to them a concept of God as transcendent reality: as a self-existent utterly independent and unlimited reality.[17] But, given Cavell's conceptualisation, God could, or so it would seem, have none of these features. If God is the world as experienced by the believer, God, by definition, could not be transcendent to the world and God could not be an independent, utterly unlimited, self-existent reality, for without men having experiences there would be no God. One is tempted to say that given Cavell's conceptualisation of God, the proper thing to say is that man created God, not God man. Obviously, however, she would not want to say anything that crude; on her conceptualisation 'creator' itself, in its religious linguistic environment, would have an esoteric meaning. Yet all the same it surely looks as if she were so committed, if we are to make anything at all out of what she is saying here.

Cavell might reply that to argue in the way I have is to neglect her earlier argument that God could not be transcendent to the world, for this would (a) itself limit God and (b) make all knowledge of God impossible so that God would in reality be incomprehensible. Both her conceptions, she could continue, and the more traditional conceptions, are unsatisfactory – after all, religion is difficult and God is a mystery – but at least her conceptions are not incomprehensible and they do enable man to make some sense out of his quest for God and some religious sense out of his tangled life. Moreover, it might be added, in speaking of God's transcendence it is not necessary to construe 'transcendence' as 'beyond the world' or 'beyond all experience'; one could instead construe it, as Marcel does, as 'that in experience which goes beyond the partial perspectives of the various scientific points of view'. In speaking of transcendence we are speaking of 'that which makes possible the experience of wholeness which we have with regard to

19

ourselves, our world and the system of intentions which enables us to give meaning to our being in the world.'[18]

There is force in such a reply, but before I return to the argument I want to continue Cavell's elucidation of a kind of esoteric God-talk. And when this is completed, it might be said, it will become evident that the above reply is adequate.

Cavell argues that it is essential that we come to see that 'the logic of "God" and of "self" are parallel, in that both seem to point to entities of which we cannot be aware, yet which are implicit in everything of which we are aware'. There is a point to the Hindu claim that God and the self, Brahman and Atman are one. The self, Cavell in effect avers, remains a puzzling and mysterious notion.[19] It 'as consciousness', she tells us, 'seems to "exist" only in a tension between two non-observable entities, world (*noumenal*) and subject, to which the act of consciousness points; which suggests that to talk about the world (*phenomenal*) is to talk about one's self in a certain way, and vice versa'.

Here we have something which is as incomprehensibly metaphysical as anything Cavell finds in the more traditional God-talk. But there is no need here for such a metaphysical jungle or for talk of 'the self' at all. Ryle, Hampshire and Williams among others, have, against our philosophical puzzlement, reminded us of the ordinary and quite adequate ways, for most purposes at least, in which we do and can talk of persons, agents and of oneself and others. There is no need to posit such a term of art as 'the self' and wonder about its relation to the world. Hampshire has made it evident in his *Thought and Action* both how easy it is to get into a Cartesian metaphysical stance and also how gratuitous and philosophically empty such talk is – as if we ourselves were not in the world. We can see, given Cavell's conception of 'the self' and God, how we could construe 'God is within us'. But such a conceptualisation not only makes 'God' incoherent but 'us' as well.

Cavell articulates well our sense of the importance of religion and something of the function it plays in our lives. She gives us – bracketing the question of whether we can make sense of her conception of what 'God' refers to and her conception of 'the self' – a good understanding of what it could mean to say that God is infinitely loving and unbounded by space and time. But, like Ninian Smart, she also recognises that religions do have

metaphysical conceptions and do make what are at least putative cosmological truth-claims. What she has not been able to
do is to give us even an inkling of what it would be like for those
alleged truth-claims to be true or even probably true or false or
even probably false. But to do this is crucial, if we are to make
sense of our religions.

It is with this line of reasoning that we can meet my un-
answered objection to my own argument. Cavell's articulation
of an esoteric strand of religious belief in effect shows these conceptions to be as incomprehensible as the traditional conceptions. It is indeed true that any conception of God, if it is
adequate to what we are talking about, must make evident the
notion that God is mysterious. But with both traditional theism
and with Cavell's conception of 'God' and 'the Self', more than
mysteriousness enters, for with them we have incomprehensi-
bility as well and no conception at all of what it would be like for
the alleged statements 'There is a God', 'God is within us' or
'God created man in His image and likeness' to be either true
or false.

As she remarks in her 'Visions of a New Religion': 'Despite
differences on other grounds, the major religions have always
been united in the conviction that what we take to be reality –
the body, physical possessions, all the things with which we
falsely and hopelessly try to identify ourselves – is illusion; that
we mistake the sum of our universe for its substance; and that
when we become "blind" to this world, considered as possession
and limitation, we will begin "to see".'[20] These are extraordinary claims yet they are indeed claims made by our
religions; moreover, for these claims to have substance, for the
very talk here of 'illusion' to have meaning, there must be
some understanding of what it would be like for the fundamental claims of religion to be true. Yet it is just in this
crucial task that Cavell, like so many others, fails us.

What I have wanted to establish by my examination of these
two different, but importantly typical, model arguments is
how sceptical claims about the very possibility of making
intelligible truth-claims in religion arise with respect to both of
them and how they have not been justifiably quieted by either
of these model arguments. In sum, problems thrown up by the
falsification challenge remain. Religions make putative truth-
claims which are integral and central to them, but it is not

21

evident how they could be genuine truth-claims at all. We must see if there is a way around this sceptical challenge.

Recently, a distinguished Danish philosopher wrote to me that he was puzzled why I bothered examining religion, for he felt that it was just too obvious that God-talk and soul-talk are meaningless to make the problem even interesting. Such scepticism is more pervasive than most people realise, though indeed many who are substantively such sceptics would object (for reasonably technical reasons) to the use of 'meaningless' here. However, it remains the case that such a scepticism is rooted in the claim that while key religious claims are taken to be truth-claims, they, in reality, are not genuine truth-claims at all. Does such a scepticism rest on a mistake? I shall argue that it does not.

2 Does Religious Scepticism Rest on a Mistake?

There are those who will say that the sceptic's very questions indicate that he has got religion all wrong and that we can, if we have a feel for what religion is all about, only be radically sceptical of such scepticism.

Paul Holmer and D. Z. Phillips, working out of a tradition deeply influenced by both Wittgenstein and Kierkegaard, try to make such a case.[1] Before I begin to examine some attempts to meet squarely sceptical challenges to religion (where the challenges are taken at face value), I want to examine this anti-sceptical argument that there is no such sceptical case to meet since it is a mistake to look for some rational foundation for religious belief or for some general standards of significance or rationality. Philosophy, such philosophers contend, cannot supply such standards as foundations for there are none; but Judaism and Christianity are none the worse off for all of that, for they neither need nor require such general criteria. No philosophical, logical or scientific sanction is required or indeed possible for religion; no sustainable case can be made for looking externally to the practices of religion themselves for criteria of intelligibility, rationality and truth in religion; outside of the discourse itself there is nothing in virtue of which we could come to see how, after all, there is a religiously viable concept of God or how fundamental religious beliefs could be seen to be true or, for that matter, false. There are, it is argued, within religion itself, good reasons for believing that there are religious truth-claims and that these truth-claims are indeed true. But they are not the type the sceptic expects and regards as relevant to the establishment of the intelligibility or truth of the claims of religion. The sceptic has a conception of what would satisfy

23

claims of intelligibility and truth for a putative truth-claim, but doubts, for religious utterances of a non-anthropomorphic sort, that either of these conditions can be satisfied. But, Holmer and Phillips maintain, the sceptic's quest is a mistaken one, for there is and can be no question of confirming 'religious hypotheses' or giving evidence for religious beliefs or displaying the facts which show them to be true or the possible facts which, if they indeed turned out to be the facts, would show them to be false. Not all beliefs need be so related to evidence and not all legitimate uses of language need be used to make confirmable or infirmable statements. Religious utterances, it is maintained, are not even of the type that should pass tests for intelligibility applicable to genuine empirical statements of fact. They do not play or even purport to play that role in religious life and to so construe them is to misunderstand their very logic.

In short, the claim is that it is not the case that the body of truths embedded in our religious forms of life are truths which require evidence or support by the facts. The 'grammar of belief' should be differently understood. We need to understand that religious beliefs are not bits of speculative metaphysics or parts of isolated language-games (esoteric forms of discourse) separated from the stream of life. Religious beliefs indeed play an important role in the lives of many people; they are closely meshed with the whole of our life and are not isolated from the facts. But they are not and cannot be assessed by the facts; rather, as Phillips puts it, they assess the facts, 'bring a characteristic emphasis to bear on the facts'.[2] They are the framework, the onlook, within which the believer meets and understands 'the fortune, misfortune, and the evil that he finds in his own life and in the life about him'.[3] To think that they are assessable by reference to the facts is utterly to confuse how religious discourse works. They regulate our lives and they have a regulative function in certain domains over what it makes sense to say, over what constitutes an explanation and over what is taken to be reasonable and unreasonable.

The thing to see, Phillips maintains, is how religious beliefs are a distinctive kind of belief. They are not conjectures, opinions, something we hold tentatively, and they are less closely linked with predictions than with conceptions of how we shall strive to live and how we view the value and significance of life. Religious beliefs are differently related to knowledge claims than are empirical beliefs. They are not beliefs which can be so generalised and systematised that we can ask for a verification of or an external check on 'religion as such'.[4]

There remains, however, on this account, a real difference between believers and sceptics, but the difference is not where I have placed it. Rather, the essential difference, Phillips claims, is the 'difference between someone who does look on his life in a certain way and regulates it accordingly and someone who has no time for such a response or who sees nothing in it'.[5] It is a critical mistake on the sceptic's part to 'think that nothing can be believed unless there is evidence or grounds for that belief'.[6] 'Belief' when we are talking about religion and when we are talking about empirical matters of fact has very different employments. Like Cavell, Phillips maintains that in coming to have a religious belief – say a firm faith in God's providence – what is most essentially involved is the viewing and regulating of one's life in a certain way and not the coming to have an opinion which is based on the weighing of evidence.[7] The difference between a believer and a sceptic is not that the believer knows something that the sceptic doesn't, but the difference is in commitment and orientation. The core confusion for sceptics and for many believers as well is to assume, indeed to hold as a very fundamental presupposition, 'that the relation between religious beliefs and the non-religious facts is that between what is justified and its justification, or that between a conclusion and its grounds'.[8] It is a pervasive mistake in thinking about religion to take it as just evident that if religious beliefs are to be sustained they must have such a foundation.

Holmer stresses, even more than Phillips, both that there is no underlying philosophical, scientific or indeed just plainly factual support for religious beliefs and that no underlying conceptual scheme or foundation for belief is needed. There are plenty of concepts actually functioning in the religious life and they are sufficient.[9] It is a mistake to think either that philosophy can supply a convincing answer to the sceptic or that it can support the sceptic's negations and doubts. Philosophy can give us no new knowledge of God nor can it even reconfirm any old knowledge to bolster up the leaky vessel of faith. In

25

this way neither philosophical theology nor philosophical atheology is possible. Philosophy cannot give us something crucial for our religious lives which Christianity or Judaism cannot; it can neither provide the ground for nor the critique of everyday religious language and practice. It is a pervasive confusion among philosophers and theologians to think that some philosophical scheme can 'become both the way of treating the meaning of the term "God" and thus of grounding it in its proper referent, and also the way of treating the question whether anything exists to which such a concept can refer.'[10] The assumption is that there is a real point to the question: Is there or is there not a God? But this is an illusion. There is no 'ultimate court of understanding' or transfield criteria of rationality or intelligibility in virtue of which this 'question' could be answered. Religion is a form of life and within this form of life there are established criteria for truth, intelligibility and rationality, but there are no transfield criteria of truth, rationality and intelligibility, in virtue of which one could justifiably claim that religious beliefs are either true or false, reasonable or unreasonable or even intelligible or unintelligible. The sceptic can have no place to stand. His very core assumptions concerning religion rest on mistakes.

II

We must put aside, Holmer and Phillips would have us understand, such philosophical preconceptions and recognise that to understand religion we must see it in its own context. In such a context we see orthodox Christians and Jews confessing their sins to God and praying to God. But, in trying to attain such a participant's understanding, it is surely natural to ask: to whom or to what are they praying or confessing when they pray or confess? Here the believer is very likely to be 'up tight', utterly at a loss to know what to say. Almost anyone who has grown up in a Jewish or Christian culture can readily play such religious language-games; that is, such a person knows how to pray and confess to God, yet even with this skill, this mastery of the language and the religious employment of the key 'pictures' used in this form of discourse, he can remain utterly sceptical about the coherence of such concepts and at sea about

26

the alleged reality for which the key religious terms stand. Such a person may have a very good understanding of how to engage in religious practices and he will, if he has such an understanding, also have a good grasp of religious language-games (forms of discourse). But the crucial point to see is that he can very well have such an understanding while remaining utterly agnostic about whether these practices make sense or whether such talk is intelligible. It may be true, as Phillips avers, that within Jewish and Christian forms of life, love of God is the primary form of religious belief, but the nagging question still remains: what are we talking about here? Where our God is not the God of religious idolatry, *what* is it that we are trying to love or are supposed to love when we love God?

With even a rudimentary understanding of the underlying structure of this discourse, it should be evident to us that God is not something which could be located and that believing in God is very different from believing that the world is round. Our 'belief in' here is indeed not the mere holding of an opinion. And it *may* even be true that for some sorts of X the only way of discovering what belief in X is like is by believing in X. But before we treat God as that sort of X, we should bear in mind that there have been countless people who have believed in God, who have thrown themselves wholeheartedly into these forms of life, and who have gradually, as they have explored the logic of their faith, come to find such beliefs not simply mysterious but incoherent. Perhaps they have made philosophical blunders in coming to think such concepts incoherent, but it is surely not correct to say of these people, as Phillips does, that they once understood and then later failed to understand. They plainly have a religious understanding and sometimes, at least, it is the case that this very religious understanding drives them into perplexity about and sometimes into a rejection of religion. Sometimes, as Phillips and Holmer show, loss of belief does not have such conceptual roots and indeed is far less intellectually defendable or (for some other cases) arguable. But there are also men with the need to believe or at least with the wish to believe who find they can no longer believe because they have become convinced that the key religious concepts of their faith are unintelligible or incoherent. And coming as it does out of religious and philosophical reflection from within this very form of life, it surely is question-begging

27

to assert that this scepticism must simply be the result of conceptual blunders.

When we believe, we must believe something. That is what Wittgenstein would call a grammatical remark. But what is it that we believe in when we love, confess to or pray to God? Is believing in God like believing in justice, i.e. is it *simply* to subscribe to a set of moral principles and to hope these principles will prevail? This, though it would relieve us of some philosophical difficulties, would hardly appear to be a characterisation of Christian or Jewish religious forms of life. Surely to believe is to do that, but is it not *simply* to do that any more than to be an M.D. is simply to be able to give first aid.

Phillips believes that one comes very close to superstition or idolatry when one treats a religious form of life as a form of life which takes belief in God to be belief in an ultimate order of fact. 'True religion', Phillips argues, does not essentially consist in trusting that a certain state of affairs is going to be the case or perhaps even in believing that a certain state of affairs is the case. Belief in God, as Phillips sees it, is *entirely independent* of the way things go. But then it becomes, to put it conservatively, doubly difficult to say what belief in God comes to. Phillips, and Holmer as well, stress how religious belief involves trust and regulating one's life in a certain way. But religious belief involves trust *in God* and that involves believing that (thinking that) there is a God. It makes no sense to say 'I trust in God but I don't think there is a God'. So we have another component in belief in God that cannot be understood in terms of trusting or anything like trusting. Moreover, the other factor does not have to do just with the regulating of one's life, for there are people who have ceased to believe or are unable to believe, who still continue to regulate their lives in very Jewish or Christian ways.

Phillips maintains, as has Norman Malcolm as well, that to give an account of belief in God one must take 'the distinction between existence and eternity seriously'. He tries to give an account of what it is to 'come to see meaning in the eternal'.[11] To understand how this links up with belief in God, it is necessary to recognise and take to heart the fact that in developed forms of the Hebrew-Christian tradition 'the conception of God is not a conception of a being among beings'.[12] Coming to see that there is a God is not like coming to see that some additional

28

being exists. It is not, as Kierkegaard paradoxically put it, like coming to see that something exists, but it is a coming to an acknowledgment of eternity. But again, what we are talking about here remains intolerably obscure. What is it to acknowledge eternity? What is it to come to understand that God does not exist but is eternal?

Let us see if we can get a purchase on this. I, of course, agree with Holmer and Phillips that the philosopher may indeed fail to understand what it means to believe in an eternal God.[13] We cannot, they point out, be confident that we, even as participants, have an adequate religious understanding even of first-order discourse. But this has an unwelcome consequence for Holmer and Phillips, for it also means that we cannot be sure that our first-order religious discourse is intact as it is and that we are only confused about the proper *analysis* of the discourse in question. I understand what it is to believe or to know that there are physical objects (e.g. sticks and stones), though I am quite unclear about the proper analysis of 'physical object', but by contrast, I am actually unclear (a) about what I am to believe in order to believe in an eternal God and (b) about the correct *analysis* of 'eternal God'. I am in doubt about the proper analysis of 'physical object' but in no doubt whatsoever about whether there are sticks and stones; however, in the religious case I am in doubt both about the proper analysis of 'God' *and* about whether there actually is or even could be such a reality.

Presumably in Christian-Jewish discourses 'eternal God' is a pleonasm, but pleonasm or not, how are we to understand such a phrase? In fact – to push the matter a little further – if we are honest with ourselves can we really rightly claim we understand it? In trying to understand and then give an account of what it is to believe in such a kind of reality, to believe in a kind of order of eternity which transforms and gives a new meaning to one's life, one should start, Phillips argues, with trying to understand what it means to speak of 'eternal love' and what role such a concept has in the stream of life. The aim of this exercise it to show how 'there is a God in this context is synonymous with seeing the possibility of eternal love'.[14]

Note first that even with respect to love between people the mine/yours distinction gets broken down into a concept of 'ours'. This is a move away from self-love to a wider reference range. The kind of love of which Christianity tries to speak is love from which no man is excluded: this is called love of one's neighbour. Phillips tries to elucidate what is meant by 'eternal love' or 'love of God' by elucidating what is meant by 'love of neighbour'. It is important to see how this love differs from self-love, erotic love, and friendship. A major difference is that love of neighbour does not depend on how things go while these other forms of love do. Self-love is thwarted where one cannot achieve what one takes to be what is good for oneself; love between people can in turn be thwarted by death, for what is such love without one's beloved? In general, friendship can cool and love can fade. It is this dependence on how things go in the world that leads us to conceptualise such love as temporal love and to contrast it with eternal love. It is in such a non-vacuous contrast that 'eternal love' gets its meaning.

A Jew or Christian is distinguished from a sceptic, according to Phillips, in believing that besides temporal love there is a 'love that will not let one go whatever happens.'[15] If one's aspirations and desires are thwarted, if one's friendships go dry and if one's love dies, one's life, if one has such a belief, is not robbed of its meaning, for *whatever* happens to one, one's life has significance. Such a love is, in the Christian tradition, called 'love of one's neighbour' and, because of its independence from conditions, it is properly called 'eternal love'. Given such a love, a man is loved not simply because he is a parent, lover, friend or even a tolerably humane man, but simply because he is a human being. Such a love is unchangeable, immune from defeat and independent of the way things go.[16] This is a love which never can deceive one because it does not depend on what happens to one. In loving in this way, one engages in self-renunciation, one loves one's neighbour no matter what he does and thus one cannot be deceived.

To love in this way, Phillips would have us understand, is to believe in God. 'To possess this love is to possess God.' This love, we are told, is 'the Spirit of God' and to possess it is to know God. Thus, in a Christian form of life, love and understanding are in some way equated. There is and can be no theoretical understanding of God and to love in a certain way is to know God.[17] In fine, to come to see the possibility of such love is to come to see the possibility of belief in God. To love in this way is to believe in God.

It is true that one could not believe in God without loving or at least having some affective attitude toward God. Knowledge of God – if indeed there is such – cannot be a purely theoretical knowledge. Kierkegaard is perfectly correct in maintaining that 'if anyone thinks he is a Christian and yet is indifferent towards being a Christian he is not one at all'.[18] But to equate belief, understanding and loving here is to confuse a necessary condition for religious belief with a sufficient one, and it is to convert atheists like myself who have such supposed exclusively Christian or religious attitudes toward love into believers by stipulative re-definition. I do indeed believe in eternal love, characterised as Phillips characterises it – though I do not like to talk in this way – but I do not believe in God. A man who really cares about humanity will indeed have such agapeistic attitudes toward his fellow men: he will love them come what may. It is a commitment which for him is categorical. And if this is what is meant by 'eternal love', he believes in eternal love. But a man with such attitudes need not believe in God or even understand the word 'God'.

To reply in the manner of Phillips that such a man is really a believer for to love in this manner is to believe in God is not to characterise the Christian religion from within, as Phillips would have us do, but to select from within this form of life *some* of the criteria for what constitutes religious belief and by *persuasive* definition to *make* them *the* criteria of 'true religion'. But this is not to keep to the pure Wittgensteinian task of conceptual analysis that Phillips takes to be the sole legitimate philosophical task. Rather it is an oblique way of doing what he thinks ought *not* to be done in *philosophy*, i.e. to advocate and to engage in apologetics.[19] And such an advocacy is all the more insidious for not being straightforward, for it appears to be a conceptual analysis of a form of language, when in reality it is the identifying of religious belief with a particular subset of religious beliefs by the simple expedient of selecting and labelling as the sole legitimate claimant for genuine religious discourse, expressive of religious beliefs, the portion of that discourse which is not 'a scandal to the intellect'. That is to say he simply ignores those bits of religious discourse which at least *prima facie* appear to contain incoherent or at least very problematical claims. (He does exactly the same thing with the concept of immortality in his *Death and Immortality*.) Here we have what in effect, if not in intention, is a form of apologetic

31

advocacy of a radically reconstructed Christianity masquerading as a neutral conceptual analysis of Christian discourse. Through an arbitrary *persuasive* definition of 'true religion', our religious options get circumscribed. The difference between a believer and a non-believer on such an account becomes simply a difference in attitude and picture preference; what appear at least to be substantial, non-attitudinal clashes between Christianity and atheism are whisked away by linguistic legerdemain. But if this is resisted there at least still appears to be room for the kind of scepticism characterised in Chapter One.

We are left, Holmer's and Phillips' arguments to the contrary notwithstanding, in the following situation. Given the type of form of life and mode of discourse that Judaism and Christianity have become, 'God', though purportedly functioning as a referring expression, is not taken to denote anything locatable. But if 'belief in God' is to be an intelligible notion, we must believe in something when we sincerely say we believe in God. But no criteria of identification have been given for identifying the referent, the alleged reality, that 'God' supposedly denotes. God is plainly not some locatable reality 'out there'. Phillips makes this evident enough. But then *what* are we talking about when we speak of God?

If God is construed as 'creator of the universe', 'pure spirit', 'pure act' or 'necessary being', we are still at a loss to identify what it is we are talking about. Thus, if a man asserts that there is indeed a necessary being, there is no way of deciding or even gaining an educated hunch whether his assertion is true or false or even probably true or false and this is, in effect, to confess that we do not understand what he is trying to claim. That is, we are trying to take it as an assertion, but we do not understand what it could conceivably assert. The trouble in the utterance 'There is a necessary being' is with 'necessary being'. We are given to understand that a necessary being is an 'independent being', 'eternal being', i.e. 'a being which could not begin to exist or cease to exist', 'a being without sufficient conditions', 'an unlimited being' and the like. But we still have no effective understanding here, for such terms are expressive of a network of notions, all of which suffer from the same conceptual difficulty: we do not know if any of them are in any way *exemplifiable*. We do not know and seem to have no way of finding out, for example, if there is an eternal being, though we

32

do know that *if* there is an eternal being, it makes no sense to ask when it started to exist or if it could cease to exist. Assuming for a moment that 'necessary being' or 'necessary existence' is in *some way* intelligible, we need to ask in a timeless, tenseless way, whether there is or could be such a being. Part of what is involved here is this: we know that if God is necessary being or existence, that if He does not exist now, His existence is eternally precluded; furthermore, it at least seems to be the case that if this necessary being does exist now, He always existed and must always continue to exist. But we still have no idea of what would or logically could constitute an answer to our putative question, i.e. whether there is or could be a necessary being. Since this is so, the concept (notion) in question is an *ersatz-*concept. Its sign-vehicle 'necessary being' purports to stand for something but actually does not. Similar arguments can be made for 'pure spirit', 'the creator of the universe', 'pure act' and the like.

Holmer and Phillips could respond that I have not really taken to heart or come to grips with their claims about the contextual (form-of-life-dependent) nature of criteria of truth, intelligibility and rationality. In my account, they could say, something is going on that is typical of philosophers, namely a confused 'craving for generality, a desire to give an all embracing unitary account of reality'.[20] But, they could add, the search for such a unit is a delusion. The distinction between 'the real and the unreal' does not come to the same thing in every context. Moreover, we have no criteria for or an independent test of whether language corresponds to reality. It is not reality which gives language its sense. It is not reality which shows which words, if any, in our discourse are empty, idling words. Rather, what is real and what is unreal shows itself in the very workings of our language, in the actual and varied uses of language in live contexts. There is no general way of talking about how language corresponds to reality and there is no general way in which we can usefully talk about criteria of rationality either. Rather, the criteria of rationality and coherence are *internal* to each mode of discourse.

I have discussed this issue elsewhere and I must be brief here.[21] First, Phillips admits that there 'will be no strict lines of demarcation between different modes of discourse at many points'. But, given this overlap, what really is the argument for

33

believing that the criteria for truth, rationality, intelligibility and evidence are contained within the particular mode of discourse in question? The very mode of discourse is not on Phillips' own account self-contained. Why, then, should we think that each mode of discourse has within itself its distinctive and self-contained criteria for truth or rationality? The concept of consistency is a part of the concept of rationality, and consistency is not utterly form-of-life-dependent. Moreover, to be rational is – though this is not all that it is – to be objective. That is, where we are talking about rational action, it is to be willing, where it is possible, to examine the evidence or reasons for a belief and to hear argument before acting or judging. Now, what in a given situation will count 'as evidence' or 'as relevant reasons' is indeed partly a function of a particular form of life but not entirely so. If someone tells me that God created the heavens and the earth, there is in English an ordinary sense of 'created' which is not utterly form-of-life-dependent and without which we would not understand that religious claim, and given this common use of 'created', I know what counts as evidence for something's being created and thus I know what, if anything, would count as evidence for that alleged claim. Because of features in common to all uses of 'created', evidence for something's being created is not utterly idiosyncratic to each mode of discourse. Moreover, we should not forget that forms of life change, drop out of existence, come into existence and overlap. We once believed in ghosts and engaged in explicit magical practices. They once were our forms of life. But our very pervasive concepts of truth, evidence and knowledge and our expanding knowledge of the world led us to criticise and finally to abandon such forms of life. Phillips' argument commits him to the *a priori* claim that it is impossible to assess rationally whole forms of life. A blunder, he would have us believe, can only be a blunder within a particular system. But to say we could have no rational grounds for criticising belief in ghosts or our own Western magical practices constitutes a *reductio* of his argument.

It is not unnatural to respond that, in arguing as I have, I neglected to consider an important page that both Phillips and Holmer take from Wittgenstein about the distinctive features of religious belief. I have spoken about the need for evidence or reasons for or against as something that must go with an assertion which could in turn be believed or disbelieved. But Phillips directly and indeed Holmer by implication have asserted that religious claims are not claims for which there can be evidence or grounds. The logic of the discourse is such that the very idea is deemed to be irrelevant.

While this may be true of some religious utterances, it has not been shown to be true of all of them. There appears to be no conceptual ban on asking (to take a key example) for the evidence for 'God created the heavens and the earth'. When someone wants to know how, if at all, it is known to be true or believed with justification to be true, he has not said something deviant or logically or conceptually odd as he would have if he had asked how we know 'Stop yelling' is true.

Phillips, however, remarks that we cannot grasp the nature of religious beliefs 'by forcing them into the alternatives: empirical positions or human attitudes.'[22] When I avow, 'I believe in God the Father, maker of heaven and earth' or 'God is in Christ' or 'God is truth', I indeed typically would be expressing an attitude, and, with respect to the first utterance quoted, perhaps in some sense I am necessarily doing that. However, this is not all that I mean to be doing; and this holds for any of the above utterances. But Phillips is no improvement on Wisdom in saying *what* this alleged more is.

In believing in any of these religious claims one believes firmly: they are unshakeable for believers, they do not think of them as conjectures or hypotheses for which the evidence is not particularly good. Rather, to be a religious believer, one must subscribe to them with one's whole heart and whole mind and, moreover, they are the framework or picture in accordance with which believers view crucial areas of their lives. That is to say, their view of birth, death, joy, misery, despair, hope, fortune and misfortune is deeply affected by this framework. Religious beliefs are firm in that they categorically regulate the believer's life in those domains on which they touch.

Religious beliefs either are or necessarily involve pictures or frameworks doing the work characterised above. But what is meant by 'framework' or 'picture' here? Plainly these terms are not being used literally, but beyond that bare acknowledgement it is difficult to know what is intended. Phillips claims that we know that when we assert religious beliefs we are not asserting empirical propositions or purely moral or purely normative claims (e.g. purely moral or normative in the way that 'You ought to think more of the feelings of others' is moral or 'Rigorous training makes good athletes' is normative). As Phillips puts it himself, religious beliefs are neither 'empirical propositions . . . [nor] human attitudes, values conferred, as it were, by individuals on the world about them'.[23] Rather the religious pictures 'have a life of their own, a possibility of sustaining those who adhere to them.'[24] Believers believe that these pictures are not pictures they can pick and choose and about whose adequacy they can make a judgement. Rather these pictures come to measure them. They simply find themselves adhering to them and subscribing to them in a quite categorical way. For them they have a value which is absolute. They are, after all, their picture of the divine for which they have and can have no substitute, since they have and can have no independent access to or notion of divinity.

This is a very odd use of 'picture' in which we are to adhere to a picture and yet can have no independent access to what is pictured. Moreover, if 'picture' *here* connotes anything similar to what 'image' connotes, there must be some notion of representation in virtue of which there must be something which the picture is a picture of. But we seem barred from any understanding of this 'something that is pictured' in religious contexts because there can be no independent access to what is pictured. And if (like an abstract painting) the picture is in no way a representation, it is difficult to understand how it can be a model and a guide.

In general, the notions of picture and framework remain so obscurely characterised by Phillips that we can make little of them or put little weight on such notions. Moreover, if these beliefs, which are also pictures or frameworks, are not, when we express them, empirical propositions or simply moral or normative ones, then, what we should say is that no alternative characterisation has been given of what they mean or how they function. Their logical status is utterly problematical. Consider:

(1) To love God is to know the truth.
(2) God is the truth.
(3) God is in Christ.
(4) I believe in God the Father, maker of heaven and earth.

None of these, according to Phillips, are empirical propo-
36

sitions and they are not analytic either. Well, then they are some other kind of proposition. Well and good. But what kind and how are we to understand them? They are said to be key religious truths, but no hint – once we exclude all evidential considerations – is given as to how we could have the slightest reason for believing them to be true or false. But if this is so, then it is difficult to understand what could be meant in saying they are truths (claims or statements) which could actually be true or false. Phillips comes perilously close to saying that truth here comes to truthfulness, that is sincerity of avowal and commitment. But then religious claims are being modelled too nearly even for Phillips' taste on moral ones. Religion, so construed, is too close for comfort to morality touched with emotion and the distinctive putative truth-claims of religion have been lost. But if Phillips backs off here, how are we to understand (1) through (4)? Presumably they have some statement-making role (constative force). But if that is so, then they have truth-values and if they have truth-values, it should be possible at least in principle to find out what their truth-values are. Phillips and Holmer have made us keenly aware of the commissive force of religious utterances: how, in sincerely avowing 'Christ is the truth and the way', I am committing myself to a norm in accordance with which I evaluate my own life and the quality of life around me. But religious utterances certainly appear at least to have a constative, statement-making force as well. But about this Phillips and Holmer are unhelpful. It seems to me that we should say of them what W. D. Hudson has said of Wittgenstein: '. . . what he seems at times to have come near to suggesting is that, because religious beliefs have commissive force, that somehow entitles us to by-pass the troublesome problem of their constative force.'[25] Furthermore, as Mitchell has recognised, that we commit ourselves quite categorically to being regulated by certain claims – in this case religious doctrines – says something about 'the pragmatics of belief' but does not imply that there cannot be evidence for or against a religious belief.[26] It only means (by definition) that for the *believer* his belief is in an important way unshakeable. If his belief is nevertheless shaken such that he no longer accepts the belief because he does not believe that it is true, he ceases (again by definition) to be a believer. But this does not mean that he cannot acknowledge that there is evidence for or against

37

religious beliefs, it is only that he, *as a believer*, is committed to treating that evidence in a certain way, namely to regarding it as not sufficiently strong to warrant abandoning his faith. But he need not contend that in some way it is logically impossible that his religious beliefs could be false. But it is impossible for him to be a believer and actually believe that his religious beliefs are false. (Again we see that even truisms can be true.)

Once we abandon anthropomorphism, it is unclear what constative force or what truth-value (if any) religious utterances have. Phillips and Holmer leave us without a clue here; indeed they are of no help beyond suggesting that we cannot establish truth here in the way we can over a question of empirical fact. But we are left entirely in the dark about how else we might go about understanding what truth-value putative religions truth-claims have and this leaves their meaning or at least their constative force problematical.

These utterances which express beliefs which are said to be pictures may very well only have what has been characterised as having a 'pictorial meaning' or a 'pictorial sense'.[27] 'There is a time machine in the basement of the Chrysler Building' is a good example. Here we have some understanding of the utterance, for we have some relevant images or pictures – we could even have a governing picture of a 'time machine' – but the utterance still could not be used to make a true or false statement. People characteristically care about (1) through (4) in the way they do not about the above utterance, but, as to their 'claims' they appear to be parallel. At the very least we have much to remain sceptical about and it does not at all seem to be the case that it has been established that scepticism rests on a mistake.

III

I do not mean to suggest that all is dross in these Wittgensteinian moves. Phillips is right in maintaining that to understand religion we must start by working from within, but we need to recall that we are agents operating with many different and overlapping modes of discourse. Working from within, we can come to recognise, by an examination of what are the implications built into a given mode of discourse, that the very

38

mode of discourse is itself incoherent. That happened with our belief in ghosts and our belief in magic and, some sceptics argue, it is with much ambivalence happening with Christian and Jewish belief. And it is this that is at the heart of much religious scepticism. It is perhaps a mistaken notion, but neither Holmer nor Phillips has shown it to be mistaken.

Holmer and Phillips, I suspect, would still protest concerning criteria for 'incoherence'. But the burden of proof is surely on them to show that our criteria for such appraisive terms are so narrow that, appearances to the contrary, we could not have had justifiable grounds for criticising our own ghostly and magical practices (forms of life). Moreover, that they were 'our practices' does not mean that we simply dumped them from within, for we have, as Wittgenstein remarks, a criss-crossed network of practices, some of which we reason in accordance with when we reason. Reasoning in accordance with this more complicated network of practices, we could come rationally to reject a whole practice or form of life.

Unless Holmer or Phillips can show that counters of this sort are mistaken, their claim that there can be no assessment of a form of life as a whole and hence no assessment of religion as a whole or Christianity or Judaism as a whole simply stands as an unjustified dogma. And with this recognition there should come a recognition that the concepts of intelligibility and rationality are not utterly form-of-life-dependent.

Christianity and Judaism as we know them commit us, if we are to be Jews or Christians, to the belief that in these religions there is an admittedly mysterious assertion of and belief in an ultimate order of fact which is different from anything sceptics can accept. But philosophical argumentation has strengthened the rather pervasive conviction among the intelligentsia that such religious beliefs are incoherent. Yet the believer believes that his belief at bottom rests on their being religious facts which together constitute an ultimate order of fact. (In that way, *pace* Holmer, his belief is thought to have a foundation.) But, as things now stand, this belief and not the sceptic's appears at least to be the belief which rests on a mistake. A Christian or Jew must, in believing in God, believe that there are true and false statements concerning divinity and some of them are of the magnitude of 'the whole universe is under the sovereignty of God'. A Christian or Jew must believe

39

that this is not just expressive/evocative, commissive or pictorial talk. But we seem to have no understanding of what it would be like for such putative statements to be true or false or even probably true or false. Thus the sceptic's case seems to be very strong indeed.

3 On the Presence of God

In trying to ascertain whether we can know that God exists or have reasonable grounds for believing that God exists or know or reasonably believe that there is a religiously adequate concept of God sufficiently intelligible or unproblematic to make belief in God a reasonable option, it is important to ask what we can make of the claim frequently made by religious people that they have experience of the presence of God. The claim is often made that the concept of God cannot be incoherent or utterly problematic and that it cannot be that we cannot reasonably believe in God because there is direct experience of God, and indeed for religious argumentation to come to anything there must be such experience.[1]

It must not be forgotten in considering such an apologetic move that there are powerful Christian institutions committed to the belief that the one true God, our Lord and Creator, can be known by what they take to be a realistic appeal to man's experience of the Divine. That is to say, it is believed that we can establish, by an honest and careful attention to what we actually experience, that there is such a Creator of the universe.

I shall not be concerned in this chapter to establish that such 'proofs' by an appeal to religious experience fail or that it is false that we have an experience of the Divine. Rather, I shall try to show that there is nothing to fail or to be proved, for the very concept of God is so incoherent, when not characterised in an anthropomorphic or immanent way, that we cannot make genuine truth-claims by its employment. We cannot, that is, make statements in which 'God' and its synonyms are used and not just mentioned, in what non-anthropomorphic religious believers would take to be a religiously appropriate way, where the putative statements in question could serve as premises or conclusions in sound arguments whose premises could be known

41

or reasonably believed to be true. In order to be able to know that God exists or to have anything like a reasonable rationale for believing in God, the concept of God must be an intelligible and coherent concept – if you will, a genuine concept. If it is unintelligible or incoherent, there can be neither inferred knowledge of the existence of God nor an experience of the presence of God, though it could be and indeed is the case that people believe they experience the presence of God. But conversely, if people really do have experience of the presence of God, then the concept of God cannot be incoherent and it cannot be the case that the truth about God's existence is unknowable or that some people at least do not in fact know that God exists. If such a claim concerning religious experience can be made out, it is clear enough that religious scepticism in all the forms characterised in Chapter One will have been undermined. However, it is pervasively felt that, while it is true that many people have religious feelings – feelings of dependency, contingency, and fearsome awe – nothing can be made of the notion of an experience of God. Among contemporary analytical philosophers, George Mavrodes in his *Belief in God* has made a determined and rigorous attempt to show that this is not so. He attempts to establish that there is a justified claim to an experience of God and that this claim has a central role in any attempt to refute scepticism. I will begin by examining his central claims.

II

Mavrodes prefaces his analysis of religious experience with some conceptual remarks about the nature of experience. Experience, he argues, is a cognitive activity necessarily involving judgements.[2] Seeing, smelling, hearing and the like are determinates of the determinable experiencing.[3] That is to say, 'Hans had an experience of (an) X' comes to, when made determinate, 'Hans saw (smelled, heard, etc.) (an) X'. And to have an experience is to have an experience of something which has existential independence of the experience itself. That is to say, 'If Hans experiences X, then X exists'.[4] We must also remember that experiencing a thing is not simply 'receiving some sort of input from that thing, being affected by that thing, or even responding (in a broad sense) to that thing'.[5] Rather, experiencing

42

always carries with it judgements and the possibility of error; that is, there are true and false perceptual judgements.

What are at least putative religious experiences are often *also* experiences of mundane objects or events.[6] But there is no conceptual anomaly here. After all, astronomers look into the eyepiece of a reflecting telescope and see, under favourable circumstances, the moon. But they also see images of the moon. Moreover, whenever the image of the moon is seen the moon is seen. But the converse does not hold: the moon may be seen, when someone looks at it with his naked eye, while the image of the moon in the reflecting telescope is not seen. But the crucial thing to recognise is that the experiencing of X can also be the experiencing of Y. Moreover, neither the man who looks into the reflecting telescope and thinks he sees the moon nor the man who looks into the reflecting telescope and thinks he sees an image is making an error in perceptual judgement. 'There is no good reason to suppose that either of them is not seeing just what he thinks he is seeing. For in these cases . . . there is an entity such as the percipient thinks he is seeing and it is associated with the input he is receiving.'[7]

Since this can be so, it can be the case, Mavrodes argues, that there can be an experience of God in connection with an experience of other objects. That is, one can encounter God in encountering the starry sky above. H could be experiencing X (something other than God) and be experiencing God as well, and yet – so Mavrodes would have it – not be in perceptual error or any other kind of error.

To flesh this out and illustrate what he is talking about, Mavrodes gives an unself-conscious and theologically un-ramified report of a person's religious experience.[8] In this report there 'was talk of hearing "the voice of God"'. The experience of God was said to have come on New Year's Eve as 'the bell rang out, telling of the inexorable and endless march of time'. The religious experience was that of the infinite greatness of God as 'the voice of God had spoken to her through the voice of the bells'.[9] Here in such a religious experience, one is said to have a personal encounter with one's Creator.

In the rather asceptic epistemological vocabulary adopted by Mavrodes, in hearing the Cathedral Bells on New Year's Eve, the hearer was affected by a sensory input coming from, on the one hand, 'various entities, such as a vibrating windowpane,

43

the sound waves in the atmosphere, or the vibrating bell' and, on the other hand, from God, as everything comes from God and depends on God.[10] The claim is that 'God is present in the input of this experience not merely in the distant past but also in the present.'[11] God here is being directly experienced in conjunction with other objects. 'God is being known in conjunction with some other object that serves as a mediator of His presence; that is, an experience of God is supervening upon the experience of some physical object.'[12] Indeed, in experiencing anything at all one might also be experiencing God.

The trouble here is not with the notion that H, in experiencing X, could also be experiencing Y, but with the kind of God-talk used in such talk of an experience of God. Mavrodes takes it as straightforward discourse whose intelligibility or coherence is not in doubt but whose truth is. That is, if Mavrodes is right, there is no justified doubt that truth-claims are being made here, but there is doubt about whether these truth-claims are true. Mavrodes tries to alleviate doubt by establishing that there is no general *a priori* reason for doubting that they are true. They fare, he would have us believe, no worse here than plain matter of fact claims. What he does not face is whether *this* God-talk is indeed the kind of talk which makes any intelligible truth-claim at all. (Note that one could have doubts about this particular kind of God-talk even if one did not have doubts about the intelligibility of God-talk generally.)

The difficulties I have in mind come out in both the report of religious discourse quoted in Mavrodes and in his own characterisation of the claims of religious experience. Consider the report first. There we have talk of 'hearing the voice of God' and we are told that 'the voice of God had spoken to her through the voice of the bells'. One would expect that this was metaphorical talk but, if so, no attempt is made to even vaguely indicate what it is a metaphor of. But no suggestion is forthcoming from Mavrodes concerning what this is or even *that* it is metaphorical talk or indeed some other kind of non-literal or analogical talk. And in his own subsequent and presumably literal talk about religious experience and God, Mavrodes uses substantially the same or similar terms as the terms used in the conceptually unsophisticated report he reported.[13]

Consider these sample sentences of such God-talk.

(1) The voice of God spoke to her through the voice of the bells.

(2) Hans really heard the voice of God in the sound of the bells.

(3) God enhanced our capacities to understand what He is saying to us and to enter more thoroughly into conversation with Him.[14]

(4) We characteristically meet God in the crises of our lives, but in reality He is always active in the world ordaining for man the proper order of incentives.

(5) Man's life is a continuous conversation with God.

(6) Men of faith live in fellowship and communion with God.

If God is conceived as Zeus is conceived or in a Zeus-like manner, then there is generally little trouble over the intelligibility of these sentences, though even on such an anthropomorphic reading (1) and (2) give us some pause because of 'the voice of the bells' or 'the voice in the sound of the bells'. What, after all, is being said here? Unless the bells were ringing out something like a Morse code, how could they speak? What would it *mean* to say they spoke or even communicated to anyone? We are at sea here unless we mean something such as the claim that the ringing of the bells aroused in us certain feelings, the having of which made it possible for us to hear the voice of God. This does not seem to be what (1) and (2) are trying to say, but if we so construe them and if we construe God on the model of Zeus, then (1) and (2) are indeed intelligible truth-claims which are just plainly false as are (on such an anthropomorphic reading) all the other sample statements listed above.

But whatever may have been the case in the biblical world, theologians and almost all believers have for a long time refused to conceive of God in such an utterly anthropomorphic way. This is reflected in our very first-order God-talk. The deliberate conceptual impropriety in Rilke's 'Does God speak Chinese too?' suggests that we do not operate with such an anthropomorphic super-star conception. We balk – and balk for conceptual reasons – at 'And how loud did God speak and in what language?' just as we balk at 'How much does God weigh?' Similarly we cannot, given our use of language, intelligibly remark, using words as they typically are used, 'God

45

speaks very rapidly and in Latin', 'People can converse with God only in Latin, French or English', 'Brett bumped into God on their first meeting', 'Jones did most of the talking when he met God in Wengen', 'You can see from the way God looks at us that our fellowship with Him is meaningful for Him too'. All this talk is meaningful talk when a person is involved, but anyone who thinks he can intelligibly and assertively utter such sentences simply fails to understand God-talk as it has developed in the Judeo-Christian religion. The Jewish and Christian God, whatever He once was, is no longer Zeus-like, except perhaps when Jews and Christians pray or engage in ritual, but certainly not when they are using 'God' reflectively though still religiously.

God, on standard Christian readings, is taken to be the Creator of the universe and, as we have seen, he is thought to be transcendent to the universe though somehow also immanent in the universe in the sense of being active in the universe. But He is still conceptualised as being distinct from the universe (the world), though indeed He manifests Himself in the universe. To speak of God, as Christians do, as being transcendent to the universe is to give to understand that (a) God is not a part of the universe, (b) God is not dependent on the universe or on anything or on any being in the universe, and (c) God is mysterious. Mavrodes, in accord with that central Jewish and Christian tradition, stresses that God is an utterly independent entity with His own existence. It is important to see what such a notion commits us to. Note that even a minimal characterisation of God gives us a notion of something than which no more exalted can be conceived. But this minimal characterisation tells us precious little until we have some idea of what, if anything, holds the title of 'that than which no more exalted can be conceived'. In trying to pin this supremely holy, utterly independent and eternal something down a little more, in trying to find some empirical anchorage for the term 'God', we are led (or at least so it would seem) into trying to conceive of a reality or of an existence which is not (as are numbers) a purely conceptual existence, and yet which is still not the idea of something or someone which might or might not exist. It is the idea of a completely independent reality, an 'Unconditioned Transcendent', upon which the whole universe depends but is in turn dependent on nothing.

46

Such a reality is not a reality that could be seen, heard, felt, met with, or encountered. Anything, as has frequently been stressed by theologians, that could literally be seen or heard would not be the God of Judeo-Christianity.[15] It isn't that God has not chosen to disclose Himself in this way but that God couldn't disclose Himself in this way. For anything which could so disclose Himself would not be God. And remember it does not count against God's omnipotence to assert that He cannot do what is logically impossible (e.g. to be both an utterly independent being and a determinate empirical reality). Empirical realities are by definition determinate realities and determinate realities are also by definition limited realities. But God also by definition is an unlimited reality. Determinate realities can at least in principle be observed, seen, heard, met, encountered or apprehended. But this cannot be the case for an unlimited and transcendent reality. Thus, at least the garden-variety determinates for the determinable 'experienced' cannot be literally used when a non-anthropomorphic God is the subject. But no other determinate for the determinable has been suggested. Since this is so, talk of 'the experience of God', 'experiencing the presence of God' or 'standing in the presence of God' is without truth-value. Yet such putative truth-claims and indeed the somewhat more abstract putative truth-claims used by Mavrodes are taken by him, and many others as well, to be true. But (1) through (6) previously quoted and (7) through (9) below – when read non-anthropomorphically – seem at least to be so indeterminate in meaning as to be utterly without truth-value.

(7) God has revealed Himself to many people in many ways.
(8) 'God is continually active in the world and is constantly impinging on the lives of men, laying on them the most terrible of demands and at the same time offering to them the most wonderful of gifts.'[16]
(9) 'God will be experienced only when He chooses to reveal Himself.'[17]

All these utterances are supposedly used to make truth-claims. That is, they supposedly have a truth-value. But one need not be a logical empiricist to recognise that if a statement has a truth-value it must be at least logically possible to find out what its truth-value is. We must at least not be conceptually barred from the possibility of uncovering some reasons or evidence for believing it to be either true or false. If we try to *assert* that P is either true or false but also try to give to understand that it is logically impossible to have any idea at all whether P is either true or false – let us call this Q – we have said, in uttering Q, something which is unintelligible. Moreover, if, *per impossible*, the above putative assertion, namely Q, was not only intelligible but true, we could never, as Mavrodes and indeed many other Christian thinkers claim we can, know such religious claims as (1) through (9) to be true, for H could know that P only if H had adequate evidence or grounds (reasons) for believing that P. But with putative truth-claims such as (1) through (9), we have no idea at all what would confirm or infirm them or be a reason for believing they are true or a reason for believing they are false. But then they can hardly be Christian truth-claims grounded in religious experience.

It might be responded, with respect to the religious utterances quoted above, that I am in effect making an unreasonable demand for a kind of literalness about God.[18] My demand is unreasonable, for this is not the way in which God-talk actually functions. Moreover, not everything that we understand do we understand in such literal terms. After all, we do manage to understand such things as Shelley's ode 'To a Skylark'. In the context of the poem, 'Hail to thee, blithe Spirit, bird thou never wert' is not unintelligible and we can come to understand difficult poets such as Donne, Yeats and Hölderlin. Not all our language either is or ought to be direct. There are things, it has been claimed, that we can only say in an oblique way. And while clarity is a great thing, there are many things that can be said but only with a limited clarity. Talk of God, given that God is a radically other, incomparable mystery, is one area of discourse that must have this feature. Moreover, we cannot prescribe in advance what is thinkable. To advance thought, particularly in very fundamental areas, we often need to grope and indeed stretch our language, stumblingly trying to say what we want to say. We must beware of bans on what it makes sense to say.

I doubt very much that there are things which can only be said in an oblique way. (After all, how could we know this? And would not this in effect be placing the kind of restrictions

48

on language that the above account is opposed to?) But I do not doubt for a moment that there are many things which are important to say which are difficult to put in a non-oblique way. Yet we should also not forget that no clear sense has been attached to 'complete clarity' and thus no sense has been given to 'limited clarity' either. But again – and in the spirit of the above objection – we do not want to set up blocks to inquiry by prescribing limits to the degree of clarity we should seek, though it is indeed also true that there are, in different areas of discourse and for different purposes, points beyond which it is pointless to seek greater clarity. The level of clarity to be sought is usually a pragmatic matter determined by interest and the philosophical programme one is engaging in, though, where questions of truth are at issue, what we should seek is to attain a level of clarity which gives us good grounds for believing what we say is true and is relevant to our concerns.

We are interested in truth in religion and criteria of truth for religious claims. Thus we do not want to remain with metaphorical or non-literal employments of language. There are in religion key claims to truth. What we want to do is find out what they are and whether they are true. This requires that we go beyond the language of metaphor and analogy. Only if some compelling argument can be given, that we, in talking of God, can only speak obliquely, will the above objection be well taken. But no such compelling argument has been given.

III

The kind of appeal to religious experience we have examined tried to treat literally what might more reasonably be thought to be pictorial or metaphorical uses of language. Perhaps, as Evans and Ramsey have stressed, pictorial and metaphorical uses of language are useful in providing us with suggestions which, if we dwell on them in a certain manner, can lead to a cosmic disclosure of 'religious truth'.[19] I shall have something to say about that later, but surely, given the difference between the context of discovery and the context of confirmation or justification, we ought, however we come by them, to be able to state in some tolerably literal way what religious truth-claims look like. I shall now attempt – moving away from the kind of

49

claim made by Mavrodes – to see if we can unearth genuine religious truth-claims.

Consider (10), (11), and (12) which are paradigmatic religious utterances.

(10) God is my Creator to whom everything is owed.

(11) God is the God of infinite mercy of whose forgiveness I stand in need.

(12) God is infinitely loving.

At least their surface grammar is such that these utterances, when employed in live religious contexts, are self-involving, indicate commitments on their utterer's part and are putative truth-claims. That is, while they have a commissive force, they also most certainly appear to be statement-making utterances. But what statements do they make, and how can we gain even the slightest inkling of whether they are true or false? What exactly, or even inexactly, are these putative statements about – for to be statements they must be about something – and what centres of interest do they reflect?

One of the first things to note is that 'God' has a prominent place in them. When, in a religious context, a religious man says something such as (10), (11) or (12) there is a presumption by people who play that language-game (do those things with words and share that form of life) that the speaker understands 'God' and knows or believes in the reality of what is being talked about, i.e. referred to by the referring expression 'God'. In this context we should not forget that while 'God' is not a normatively neutral term, 'God' still is a referring expression, though we must understand that there are referring expressions of diverse types. They may be names, pronouns, definitive descriptions, indefinite descriptions, or demonstrative descriptions. Thus, as Bishop I. T. Ramsey puts it, 'if genuine belief in God is being claimed . . . the commitment involved must be more than the taking up of an attitude to the world. It must arise as a response, in a situation where we are aware of an objective referent.'[20] In using (10), (11) or (12) properly, as part of some connected discourse, the believer is trying to employ 'God' referentially. He presupposes that it has an objective referent. Without this presupposition his faith would be in vain.

However, it is just here that we have a key problem. Once we abandon anthropomorphism in which 'God' is construed like

50

'Zeus', what is this objective referent that 'God' stands for? There are men with the attitudes and depth experiences of a believer who know that 'God' is taken to be a referring expression by believers, yet they can make nothing of God. They have no clue concerning what is being talked about beyond an understanding that (a) certain very distinctive attitudes are involved and (b) they have an ability to shuffle around in determinate and mutually expected patterns certain putatively synonymous or near synonymous terms such as 'Creator of the universe', 'unlimited being', 'self-existent reality' and the like, where what counts or could count as an objective referent for these terms is as puzzling as what counts as an objective referent for 'God'. Ordinarily, if a term has an objective referent it is, at least in principle, possible to identify its referent. Consider here 'Mary', 'Montreal', 'the Eiger', 'overly shy', 'red blood corpuscles', 'aggressive behaviour', 'secondary drives', 'tardiness', 'genes' or 'alpha particles'. Here we have a mixed bag, including some very theoretical terms, but they all share the same fate of being terms where we can specify, if we understand their use, what answers to them and what does not. There is a determinate and specifiable reality, or determinate and specifiable realities, for which these terms stand, which a person who understands their use can pick out or otherwise identify; that is, they have criteria of identity and are employed to make identifying references such that it can be ascertained what is being talked about. And indeed if an expression does function referentially this must be true. But it is entirely unclear what it would be like to identify, what it is that 'God' refers to where 'God' is employed non-anthropomorphically.

There are a number of standard replies which typically are made at this juncture. I shall consider them and assess their adequacy. One very standard one is to say that to talk in this way is illegitimately to assimilate God-talk to talk of finite and indeed discrete material realities. But to do this, it is claimed, is to miss the whole point of Tillich's repeated arguments that God is not a being among beings, a finite and determinate reality. To so construe 'God', Tillich claims (as does Copleston as well), is to misconstrue how 'God' is used in the Judeo-Christian tradition. God is conceived to be invisible and transcendent. The early Christian fathers were perfectly clear about this. Athanasius tells us that God is 'by nature invisible and

51

incomprehensible, having His being beyond all created existence . . .'[21] And still earlier Origen asserted that 'According to strict truth God is incomprehensible and inestimable . . .'[22] Moreover, God is not the sort of reality of which it is possible to say *what* He is. As the theologians of the Cappadocian group put it 'faith is competent to know that God is, not what He is'.[23] God is such that 'it is impossible to express Him and more impossible to conceive Him'.[24] There is no comparison, Hilary of Poictiers tells us, 'between God and earthly things . . . the ineffable cannot submit to the bounds and limitations of definition'.[25] Thus it is evident enough that at least with the Church Fathers, 'God' – even in that early period – was *not* construed anthropomorphically as a being among beings. God, even then, is not Zeus-like. Granted that 'God' is not a referring expression of the same type as 'Mary', 'Montreal' or 'genes', still, as a referring expression (an expression employed referentially), it must be an expression which makes an identifying reference. And granted that we cannot identify God by ostension, that we cannot pick Him out as we can distinguish and pick out, as we look up at the appropriate mountain range, the Eiger, the Monk and the *Jungfrau*, still 'God', as a referring expression, must refer to something identifiable. This does not mean something must actually exist for a genuine referring expression to refer to, but that we must be able at least to conceive, as with 'golden mountain', what would count as an objective referent for the term. As Ronald Hepburn points out, where an expression, such as 'God', 'refers to an existent of some kind, one needs to provide not only a set of rules for the use of the expression but also an indication of how the referring is to be done . . .'[26] Given that God is said to be invisible, incomprehensible and transcendent, no existent among existents but a distinctive kind of existence, how are we to understand this talk and understand what identifying reference 'God' makes or what is the supposed objective referent of 'God'?

This is our old sceptical query about God-talk again and in seeing how another stab might be made at answering it, we can exhibit another standard response to our point about the lack of a coherent conception of what counts as an objective referent for 'God'. We need, it has been said, to recognise that the concept of God is not only attitude-expressing and attitude-evoking but that it is a metaphysical concept as well. To under-

52

stand what God-talk is really all about and to see that God-talk is more than metaphor, since it involves genuine truth-claims as well, we must understand the metaphysical conceptions involved. Consider the following bits of metaphysical religiosity:

(13) God is being itself, the ineffable ultimate reality.
(14) God is the Unconditioned Transcendent on which everything else is dependent.
(15) God is ultimate reality.
(16) God is ultimate reality, that incomparable and wholly other source and unity of all beings.

All of these are presumably identity statements and indeed statements which, if true, are necessarily true in the same way that 'A puppy is a young dog' is necessarily true. But we cannot know that this is so for (13), (14), (15) and (16), because phrases integral to them, such as 'being itself', 'ultimate reality', 'ineffable ultimate reality', and 'Unconditioned Transcendent', have no use and are so utterly problematic that we do not understand what is being said when people make such utterances. 'God' is perplexing but familiar, but these phrases are still more perplexing and have no fixed use in any form of life.

It might be responded that this objection and this attitude rests on a kind of linguistic and conceptual conservatism that is intellectually stultifying. As Thomas Kuhn has shown, the great conceptual revolutions in science have been such that for the revolutionaries it was almost as if they were talking nonsense.[27] The resources of the language had to be stretched to accommodate insights – initially highly inarticulate insights. It is easy to represent such thought as nonsense and thus to stifle creativity and stifle conceptual innovation which may be rooted in genuine discovery and insight.

I am in complete agreement with the general thrust of this response. We must beware of rejecting as nonsense everything presented in an odd, infelicitious, and paradoxical way; and we must beware, as in the above case, of simply dismissing claims which use an inflated and perhaps even bombastic and obscure idiom. We must try to understand the context in which they are used, the role they play in the system of thought in question and to what they are applied. Do they in reality evoke any insight or in this case (to use Ramsey's phrase) 'cosmic

53

disclosures'? We need to do this to block off a shallow scepticism which would in effect block inquiry and a search for truth.

However, we must do a complicated balancing act here. For it is also the case that much nonsense and rationally pointless obscurantism has come from metaphysical and theological thought and systems. In accommodating the appropriate latitudinarian attitudes expressed above, we must beware of rejecting the critical insights of Moore, Ayer and Wittgenstein.

Perhaps theologians such as Tillich and MacQuarrie, both of whom engage in such being-talk, do convey major and systematic insights concerning the truth-claims of religion. We surely must try to understand, from the inside as it were, what they are up to. But externally we should raise the following line of sceptical argumentation as well.

'Being itself', 'ultimate reality', 'wholly other source and unity of all beings', 'Unconditional Transcendent' are all supposedly referring expressions. That is, it is assumed they stand for something and can make an identifying reference. But then they must have an intelligible opposite. Consider, for example, 'being itself' in (13). If such obscurantist talk helps characterise what 'God' actually means, i.e. gives us something of the cognitive import of the term, it must in some way indicate something about God, something about how God is a different kind of reality, or what it means to say that God is ultimate reality. But, to do this, 'being itself' must contrast with something else. But in turn, to do this we must be able to distinguish being itself from something else; being itself must make an identifying reference. Yet how is being itself to be identified? We seem at least simply to have the phrase and nothing else.

It will not help to say that the opposite of 'being itself' is 'nothing' for 'nothing' in ordinary discourse is not employed as a referring expression, and if we try to regiment language and make 'nothing' function as a referring expression then we are led to the absurdities that Lewis Carroll satirised. If Nobody passed the messenger on the road, then Nobody would have arrived before the messenger. To try to treat 'nothing' as a name or a referring expression is to get involved in the absurdity of asking what kind of a something, what kind of *a* being, or what kind of being, is nothing. But if 'nothing' does not function as a referring expression, 'being itself' will lack designative or descriptive significance, for it will have no intelligible opposite

54

and will not at all help us to understand what we are talking about when we speak of God. I shall not go through the analysis but very similar points could readily be made about 'ultimate reality', 'unconditioned transcendent' and the like. These terms of theological art do not succeed in having genuine descriptive or designative significance and thus they do not help us to understand what we are talking about when we speak of 'God'.

It is natural enough to respond that this is not so, for 'Unconditioned Transcendent' and 'incomparable and wholly other source and unity of all beings', for at least these terms, opaque as they are, suggest that whatever God is, He is not like us, or the towering mountains, or the starry sky above, or the moral law within. He is a radically different *kind* of reality. At least we know that much. But this claim has the difficulties associated with the *via negativia*. If we only know what God is *not*, we have no inkling *at all* of what He is positively and we do not at all understand what we are talking about in talking about God, for in only knowing what we are *not* talking about, we do not know or even have the slightest idea how we could find out whether we are actually talking about God or nothing at all. To have a grasp of the concept of God we must have some positive characterisation of God.

Alternatively we may argue, as Alastair McKinnon has, that 'God' is used in some contexts which are religiously appropriate 'as a marker for "the Ultimate Reality", whatever that should prove to be.'[28] But here we have something wholly indeterminate and not something which must be the case. The world could not fail to have some order. But to assert that there must be an ultimate reality (a) is not to assert something which we have any good reason to believe must be necessarily true and (b) we do not have any reason, given McKinnon's reading of 'ultimate reality', even to think that any determinate claim has been made, for we have no idea of what we are talking about in talking of 'ultimate reality'.

Exactly the same thing is true if we say that there must be a world-ground. There is a sense in which the world must have some order, though there is no conceptual necessity that it must have any one particular order, including the particular order it has. But no reason at all has been given why the world must have a world-ground. In fact it is entirely unclear what is meant by 'world-ground'. Like 'being itself' and 'ultimate reality', it appears at least to be a Holmesless Watson. We have two more *ersatz* referring expressions which do not at all enable us to know what we are talking about when we speak of God.

Such metaphysical interpretations of God-talk seem at least to lead us into a swamp. They do not at all enable us to understand how or that 'God' has an objective referent. They purport to give us a sense of what objectively God-talk is really all about, where it is no longer a figurative metaphorical or mythological mode of speech, but in reality (or so it seems to me) they fail to do so. But perhaps I am being too woodenly literal; perhaps I have not cast around long enough for an intelligible reading of such metaphysical discourse – a reading which would show what genuine and indeed profound truth-claims certain key religious utterances really make? Religion is not meant to be something which is clear and free of paradox. And perhaps in trying to show what is involved in 'religious truth-claims', one cannot avoid making some paradoxical claims. But all the same, the difficulties I raised with 'being itself', 'unconditional transcendent', 'ultimate reality' and 'ground of the world' seem at least to be very real difficulties. Just what is being claimed here? Do we really understand what, if anything at all, we are talking about? Until and unless we have some tolerably straightforward answers here, there are no nearly sufficient reasons for rightly believing that such utterances as (13) through (16) are coherent claims which might just possibly be true. Rather, what appears at least to be the case, is that they are so incoherent that they couldn't even be true. To this it might be responded that appearances are deceiving. These metaphysical statements appear to be incoherent because we have not thought through in the right light the claims of ineffability made by such claims as (13) and (16). After all, religion speaks of an 'ineffable ultimate reality'. And from Plotinus, through the Church Fathers, to modern Neo-orthodoxy, we have come to see, in one way or another, that it is being claimed that God necessarily surpasses all our conceptualisations or notions of what God is. God is an ineffable and ultimately incomprehensible reality. Our metaphysical terms try to suggest that this is so, but they can only do so in a misleading and oblique way. To fail to see that this must be so, is to confuse 'true religion' with 'idolatry'. We must recognise that there are some things which are literally unsayable or inexpressible, but are nonetheless given in those experiences of depth where man confronts his own existence. The claim in sum, is that there are 'ineffable truths' which cannot be put into words. People with the proper depth experiences understand them, and understanding them come to have an understanding of what it means to speak of God, but what they understand and know to be true cannot in any way be literally expressed.

Tempting as it may be to talk in this way, it still seems to me that such doctrines of ineffability are incoherent. If 'God' stands for an *ineffable* ultimate reality, then nothing can be predicated of that reality and indeed nothing literal can be said about God. But to say this is to give to understand that no sentence about God or sentences in which 'God' occurs in a religious and non-anthropomorphic linguistic environment can be employed to make true or false assertions or to express facts. Thus, on such an understanding of God-talk, 'the world is dependent on God' or any other God-sentence cannot literally make a true or false statement. It *appears* to be a bit of language we can employ assertively but if what the ineffability thesis claims holds about God, we cannot so employ it in that domain.

On such a thesis, such sentences cannot, appearances to the contrary, be employed metaphorically or symbolically. If an utterance P is metaphorical, this entails that it is *logically possible* for there to be some literal statement Q which has the same conceptual content or at least has a very similar conceptual. context. If it makes sense to say that P is a metaphor it *must* make sense to say *what* it is a metaphor of. Thus it is incoherent to claim that all God-talk is metaphorical and that there can be no literal statements of religious truth but only 'the felt truth' given in an awareness of the ineffable God-head.

It may be countered that even if talk of God-talk being metaphorical or symbolic is dropped, the central core of the ineffability thesis remains untouched, for it is simply the thesis that some people at least can know what P means and indeed know that P is true though P cannot even in principle be expressed or publicly exhibited. God can be known, even though the concept of God is incoherent and our very talk of God infected with this incoherence.

57

Can we know, as the ineffability thesis affirms, anything which is *logically* impossible to express or to exhibit in any statement? This is not a possible kind of knowledge, for if P is known, then P is true, since it is not possible to *know* what isn't true. But since only statements can be literally true there could then be no 'inexpressible knowledge'. Furthermore, for something to have a meaning or to have meaning, it must have a use in a language or in some system of notation. This partially specifies what it means for something to have a meaning or have meaning even when we speak of the meaning of a concept, for we use 'concept' to signify what is expressed by synonymous expressions in the same or different languages or systems of notation. That is, 'a concept' is what is expressed by those synonymous expressions. But only if something has meaning or has a meaning can we understand what it means, so we cannot understand something which is inexpressible *in principle*; there would be nothing to be understood, for there would be nothing that is meaningful.

Even if we admit (mistakenly I believe) the above argument to be less than decisive because it assumes what has not been conclusively established, namely that a 'private language' (Wittgenstein's sense) is logically impossible, there are still other considerations which refute the ineffability thesis.[29] If someone knows something that is literally in principle unsayable, inexpressible, incapable of being shown or in any way exhibited, then there can be no communicating this 'knowledge' and thus it cannot justifiably be *said* that it is *God* that is experienced, known, or encountered. And it cannot be justifiably said that it is God in which we place our trust or to whom we owe unquestioning obedience. What is unsayable is unsayable is a significant tautology. Given the thesis that God, as the utterly ineffable (the 'utterly other reality'), is indescribable, then the very possibility of expressing one's knowledge or belief in this domain is ruled out. So, given such a thesis, there could be no confessional community or circle of faith. The ineffability thesis is reduced to the absurd by making it impossible for those who accept such a thesis to acknowledge the manifest truth that Christianity is a social reality.

If what I have argued about ineffability and the *via negativa* is substantially correct, it cannot be the case that it is correct to say or think, as some theologians have, that the paradoxical nature of God-talk shows the 'inexpressibility of religion' – the inexpressible reality that paradoxical religious language is designed to point toward – and it cannot be correct to say that the religious use of language helps 'point people beyond human concepts' to the inexpressible.

Finally, it cannot be correct to say that even contradictions in the use of religious language are valuable in showing that certain concepts do not apply to God and to loosen us up to the recognition that God is the inexpressible.[30] This cannot be correct for 'the inexpressible' is a contradiction in terms. If that is what religion is about it is plainly an illusion and atheism is not only the only reasonable position to take, it is the only intelligible position. If it is the case that we must speak of the 'inexpressibility of religion' in a non-hyperbolic way, then religion rests on an illusion. If we claim, as T. R. Miles does, that 'to say that God is transcendent is to emphasise the non-applicability of any concept whatever . . .', then what needs to be recognised is that this is in effect to give us to understand that 'God' is a meaningless term.[31] If God-talk has a totally 'incomprehensible outreach', then there can be nothing at all to God-talk. Just to the extent that it is literally incomprehensible, it is also utterly empty and of necessity devoid of content and value.

In arguing as I have about ineffability, I am not denying the actuality of a familiar enough experience of religious people, but I am attempting to undercut a certain metaphysical interpretation that is given to that experience. It is common enough for the man who has an intense religious experience to say that what he finds in his experience is 'beyond words' or is 'inexpressible'. I am not for a moment suggesting that in saying that he is 'talking nonsense', though he would be talking nonsense if in saying that he was urging the kind of ineffability thesis I have examined above. But what he should be understood as making is the sensible and unmetaphysical claim that the intensity of his experience is such that he cannot find words (literally, as a matter of fact) to express it. It is like saying of a pain 'that pain is indescribable' but this is not to say that no concept whatever applies to that pain.

4 Some Theological Counters

We have seen that neither talk of God as being itself and the like nor claims about God being an utterly other ineffable reality will help us to make sense of religion. Rather, they lead or at least should lead us to the belief, as Feuerbach phrased it, 'that nonsense is the essence of theology.' In sum, we should recognise that in these directions it is unlikely to be the case that we can make sense of non-anthropomorphic God-talk or understand how it could be that the putative truth-claims of religion could be genuine truth-claims. But to let the case for scepticism rest here is a mistake, for there are more sophisticated attempts to exhibit the relevance of experience to God-talk than those we have hitherto examined. I have in mind here the work of Donald Evans, Ninian Smart, Ian Crombie, Ian Ramsey and Gordon Kaufman.[1] They have all, though in somewhat different ways, given us complicated and sophisticated analyses of the concept of God and of the experiential bases of God-talk – arguments which do not fall prey to my earlier arguments about the incoherence of talk of experiencing the presence of God. I cannot examine all their arguments in their variety and detail but I want to face some of the core considerations here.

I shall begin by exposing what I take to be a cluster of unsolved problems emerging from Ninian Smart's effort to demythologise claims made about the ineffability of God. After making arguments against what I have labelled the ineffability thesis which cut in the same direction as my arguments, Smart goes on to try to show that there is a more moderate thesis which is defensible and which makes an absolutely indispensable claim for any viable account of religion.

Smart recognises that for 'God' to be intelligible, God cannot be literally ineffable and indescribable. It must be the case, for

61

religion and God-talk to make sense, that 'the religious ultimate' – for Christians, God – must be mediated in some mode of
experience and if it is mediated 'in some mode of experience,
then it is in some degree describable.'[2] For 'God' to be intelligible, Smart contends, God must manifest Himself in a
determinate mode of revelation or human experience, yet it
must also be the case that God necessarily transcends these
manifestations. Reflective faith uses models to concretise and
anchor God-talk but it always checks anthropomorphism with
the indispensable 'notion of an incomprehensible outreach
beyond the manifestations of God . . .'[3] If we are attuned to
God-talk, if we have a genuine understanding of religion, we
will recognise 'that in the very manifestation of the religious
ultimate we are able to see that it is mysterious and not fully
to be comprehended'.[4]

Now there is indeed a sociological remark about religious
believers which is crucial here and indeed is, as far as I can
ascertain, a true descriptive statement concerning people,
namely the claim (as Smart puts it) that religious people
typically view (look on) certain experiences, events, sacraments,
etc., as manifestations of the unseen, and indeed the unseeable
and 'as thus having a transcendent outreach beyond the manifested'.[5] That this is how religious people tend to react seems
evident enough and that this is crucial for their mode of discourse also seems evident. But what is not so evident is whether
this way of thinking and talking makes sense. Is such talk, after
all, intelligible?

Smart thinks that it is. There are others who remain sceptical.
In trying to get a purchase on this, reflect on how we are to
understand 'having a transcendent outreach beyond the manifested'. This, for some, may be a powerful emotive phrase but
how are we to understand what it is about or *do* we understand
what it is about? Is this simply another way of saying what
Crombie says, namely that a crucial function of the word 'God'
is to show the direction of reference beyond the world and that
it refers to something outside human experience and life?[6] If
this is the case, we must tread very carefully. There are indeed
things which are outside my experience. I do not know what it
would be like to vacation on the Albanian coast or work and
live in new Cuba. But these are experienceable and indeed
experienced. What, however, could be meant by 'something's

62

being altogether outside human experience and life'? How could we discover such limits, how would we know it if we came upon such limits? We seem at least to be asking for what could not be had here; to know that there were limits here would we not have to be able to think and experience beyond them? But if this were so, then they wouldn't be the limits of what is experienceable or thinkable.

This surely seems at the very best to be a quagmire; there seems to be no sensible claim behind such problematic talk. Similar things should be said for 'reference beyond the world'. What is it to get beyond the universe? 'Beyond' could hardly be used spatially. But how then is it used or indeed how could it be used? We are not told. Is the universe like some great egg, earth or sun that literally has limits? If so, what are they and how would we go about determining what the limits of the universe are? And if all this talk is metaphorical, parabolic, or analogical, what is the literal claim for which such talk is metaphorical, parabolic, or analogical? If there is none, as appears to be the case, then talk of 'metaphor', 'parable' or 'analogy' in this context is without a determinate sense. Something cannot be a parable if it is not at least in principle possible to say what it is a parable of. Similar considerations hold for metaphor and analogy.

'Transcendent outreach beyond the manifested' again has similar difficulties. My anger may manifest itself in aggressive behaviour and we know how to 'get behind' this to find out what causes it. Here the metaphor 'get behind' is perfectly in place. We know how to cash it in in terms of onsetting conditions such that when these conditions occur for a person like me, angry behaviour will occur. But where what is 'beyond the manifested' has no further reality in the world but supposedly a reality of an utterly different kind not spatially related to realities in the world or even spacio-temporally locatable, what work is 'beyond' doing? God is somehow, and essentially, screened from the world, but still manifested in the world. But 'screened' is another metaphor we cannot translate in this context. In ceasing to be a Zeus-like concept, God cannot literally be said to be 'out there', 'up there', 'down there', 'within' or anything of the sort. But the phrases Smart uses depend for their intelligibility on such rejected anthropomorphic associations. Without them they are as inapplicable and as senseless

63

as '3 p.m. on the sun'. It may well be that Christians believe that their unseeable God is, while transcendent to the world, still 'mediated somehow to human experience' in revelation, conversion, contemplation, or ecstasy. But for this to be an intelligible belief, for this to be something more than an obscure way of talking, there must be some way of indicating what it would be like for this to be so or not to be so, so that we would have some idea what it would be like to believe, doubt, know, think, or even wonder whether this is so. (We cannot even wonder if P is so unless we understand what P claims, e.g. 'I wonder if Tuesday is telegraphed'?)

In turn Smart might reply that such objections simply assume that for God to be real, God must be a different *kind* of reality from that which God actually is. But this, he could argue, is question-begging, for by definition 'God is qualitatively different from anything in the world', 'God transcends the world and is thus not discoverable in space and in time' and 'God is non-identical with the world and persons existing in the world'. With my above difficulties I only in effect bring out that God is not an object in the world.

That is not at all 'all that I bring out', for what I bring out is that since God is not such an anthropomorphic being and given that he is alleged to be some other radically different sort of reality, no sense has been given to talk of God's manifesting Himself in the world. If we set aside our anthropomorphic images and concentrate on 'the kind of reality' that God is said to have, we can make no sense of this talk of manifestations of God.

I shall come at this in a different way by following out a remark made by Smart. God is not, Smart tells us, absolutely incomprehensible, for what a religious person takes to be a manifestation of God must of necessity, as a manifestation, be of some determinate character. But then God must be of some determinate character too and thus not absolutely incomprehensible. But, if this is what is being said, then it cannot be the case that God is utterly transcendent to the world and is not discoverable in space and time.

However, it still might be the case, Smart surely would say, that God is not to be identified with these manifestations and in part lies beyond the world. But what are we to make of 'in part' in this context? It sounds as if we are saying something of

64

the same type as 'the Lake of the Woods lies in part in Canada but another part lies in the United States'. But if we try to construe the 'in part' similarly in the God-sentence, then we hardly have located a sense in which the 'transcendent part' of God – a God supposedly also utterly unchangeable and indivisible – is a qualitatively different, distinct kind of reality in principle unseeable and non-locatable in space and time. If alternatively we construe the 'in part' metaphorically, then our earlier difficulties come trouping back in. However, if to avoid anthropomorphism, we try to conceive of God as being utterly transcendent, as 'wholly other in character from us (and from features of our world), we have no means of claiming that the words used . . . have any sense at all. For if they apply in a totally different way to God, their use is not merely unintelligible, but represents a radical equivocation.'[7] Smart wants to say that we somehow can describe our non-anthropomorphic God. But he has not managed to show how this can be done or what (if any) religiously appropriate sense we can give either (a) to 'God transcends the world' or (b) to 'God is mediated in our experience by his manifestations though still transcendent to these mediations and indeed the world'.

What is troubling here is not 'that the descriptions we use of the religious ultimate are inadequate'. The difficulties are far more radical than that. Smart rightly points out that descriptions can be true and still inadequate. If all the fish in the Rhine are being killed by pollution, I can truly say that some fish were killed in the Rhine. What I say is true but thoroughly inadequate. But where we have a conception of an inadequate description we must, if 'inadequate' is to qualify 'description', have a conception (though not necessarily a precise conception) of an adequate description. Words like 'inadequate' must make a non-vacuous contrast if they are to have a meaning. If anything and everything that can even be conceived of is said to be an 'inadequate X', then to speak of 'an inadequate X' is just a cumbersome way of speaking of an X; 'inadequate' doesn't even qualify X and does no descriptive work. Now in the case of my description of the fish pollution situation in the Rhine we know what a more adequate description would look like and it is because of this that we can say that my description was inadequate. But the religious case is radically different. There, *our very best* descriptions are said to be inadequate and we have

65

no idea of what it would be like to give descriptions which would be more adequate. In fact what we want to say is that it is inconceivable that there will be or can be descriptions which will in any fundamental way make up for our inadequate descriptions and give adequate descriptions. But this only attests to the fact that we are misusing talk of 'adequate' and 'inadequate' descriptions. If no conceivable description would be adequate, no description is inadequate either.[8]

It may be replied that we can still say that any description of X will be inadequate, meaning by that that such descriptions are inadequate by comparison with other sorts of things (simple sorts of things) which can be described more adequately. Thus there are entities of type Y (say marbles) which can be more adequately described than entities of type X (say landscapes). By comparison with Y all descriptions of X are inadequate. But even here to recognise this about X and to make a comparison with Y, it must be the case that the *logical possibility* of a more adequate description of X is not ruled out, for we must, to compare X and Y, have *some idea* of what it would be like to do for X what we did for Y, such that we could, as far as logical possibilities are concerned, give an adequate description of X. Marbles, for example, can be more easily and adequately described than hazy English landscapes. But we know the kind of detail we would have to give to describe a landscape as adequately as a marble. But this is not the position we are in with respect to God. He is alleged to be a different *kind* of reality concerning which we do not and cannot know how to perfect our descriptions.

It will not help to say, as Ninian Smart does, 'there is no *a priori* reason why God should not show himself to be beyond adequate description (much as the nuances of a musical composition can show themselves to defy full description in our language)'.[9] The analogy is ill-conceived because even if we cannot adequately describe the nuances of a musical composition in our language, we can fully describe them in another language, namely in musical notation. So we still know what an adequate description would look like. But if, in turn, it is said that neither that nor any conceivable notation would give an adequate *description* of the nuances of the musical composition, then we are back to our original difficulties, for then 'adequate description', 'inadequate description' and 'full

66

description' are being deprived of any coherent meaning. And it is senseless to ask that any description be the same as the experience itself. That is like asking that a description of X cease being a *description* of X and become X itself. Of course there is a difference between the musical composition and any description of it, but for all that the description need not be inadequate. Moreover, in the musical composition case, both the descriptions and the music are perfectly available to us to compare. But in the transcendent God case, it is just such a comparison that cannot be made. We have our numinous experiences (feelings of awe, fear, dependency, finitude) and our language but no transcendent God *directly* experienceable and independently empirically available to us.

So we are left with the problem Smart sets for us but does not solve. Religious people want to be able to claim intelligibly that God is indeed transcendent to the world and as such utterly unseeable and not even a possible datum of experience, yet this transcendent reality is still thought to be manifested in the world – and as such remains to some degree describable. Smart has not been able to show how we can make sense of this core idea which appears, when we probe it a little, to be incoherent. But he has shown how central it is to Judeo-Christian thought.

II

I want now to look at another attempt to make sense of this central conception and by doing so to establish, contrary to what I have argued, that fundamental religious claims can be genuine truth-claims.

Starting with an articulation of a certain cluster of experiences he calls 'depth-experiences' and a conception of faith in God, which he thinks is best understood by reference to those experiences, Donald Evans attempts to show how God-talk is intelligible in such a way that we have in experience the clues as to what it could mean to believe in a 'hidden personal being called "God"', a being who is indeed transcendent to the world and a being than which no greater, no more exalted, can be conceived.[10] The thing we need to ascertain here is whether these experiences do give us an understanding of the notion of a manifestation of a completely independent transcendent

67

reality upon which the whole world depends but which is itself dependent on nothing.

Numinous experience – the sort of experiences so extensively characterised by Rudolf Otto in his *The Idea of the Holy* – is one of Evans' key examples of a type of depth-experience which can be given such an interpretation. Suppose I look out at a range of mountains or a sunset at sea. If in doing so I come to have an 'overwhelming feeling of awe, a sense of my own littleness coupled with a joy in being so much alive and a dumbfounded wonder at the mystery of beauty', then I am having a numinous experience.[11] I am also having a numinous experience if a Gandhi-like or Aloyasha-like man evokes in me a sense of 'reverence or self-abasement' or arouses in me feelings of bewilderment or exhilaration.

Evans is perfectly aware that these experiences can be understood in a purely secular manner, but, he tells us, 'the man of faith interprets the depth-experience as a revelation concerning both man and God'.[12] These depth-experiences do not, he believes, just show in man a mysterious depth, a capacity for awe, self-abasement, exaltation and wonder, but they also attest to the fact that they can be read as 'a revelation of God, the hidden personal being who reveals His inner nature through the numinous sunset or saint'.[13] But the problem is what does it *mean* to 'interpret the depth-experience as a revelation of God'? What could this mean?

Talk of these numinous experiences is perfectly intelligible but also perfectly empirical and secular. And talk of 'interpretation' in ordinary contexts makes evident sense; we know what it means to interpret, look on, or read X as Y and we understand seeing X as Y and viewing X as Y. We can fill in these variables with several ranges of values. But what does it mean to speak of a 'revelation of God' or of seeing or viewing or looking on something as a 'revelation of God'? Until we have some understanding of that phrase, we are utterly stumped. But it is just such a notion that we are at sea about in trying to understand the objective referent of 'God' or in understanding how religious claims could be genuine truth-claims. Evans claims that 'the depth-experience provides a context for meaningful language concerning God' but it is quite unclear how this can be so.[14] It isn't that I want to deny that experiences can be interpreted in different ways. That this is so is perfectly evident, but I question whether we have in this case a sufficient understanding of what we are to interpret our experience as to make such an interpretation possible. (We at best have a pictorial sense of 'the such' here.) Evans would have it that 'religious faith is a practical commitment to an interpretation of depth-experiences as divine revelations' and that the meaning of our descriptions of God 'cannot be understood in abstraction from elusive and mysterious depth-experiences . . .'[15] But while these depth-experiences may be a *necessary condition* they are not a *sufficient condition* for having an understanding of 'God'. We may even know how correctly to employ God-talk – we do not repeatedly make deviant utterances in this domain – and still remain, though we have these depth-experiences and dwell on them carefully, without a clue as to what it *means* to speak of this infinite, unlimited Being transcendent to the world. We could perfectly well understand that believers believe that such talk has truth-value and yet not have the slightest idea what its actual truth-value is or the slightest idea how to go about determining its truth-value.

It is the case, as Evans puts it, that we have for a variety of matters onlooks, i.e. 'I look on X as Y' as in 'I look on alcoholism as a disease' or 'I look on capitalism as an evil'. (Often we can, for an onlook, substitute for the formula 'look on X as Y', 'see X as Y', 'regard X as Y' or 'think of X as Y'.) And sometimes an onlook expresses a world view as in 'I look on matter as the ultimate reality' or 'I look on the world as the creature of God'. Moreover, in many instances, onlooks 'are practical, putatively-objective and serious. They are appraised in such terms as profound/superficial, reasonable/unreasonable, true-to-reality/mistaken, adequate/inadequate, coherent/incoherent.'[16] Furthermore, onlooks are something for which there can be evidence and reasons, though it is 'difficult to abstract and state the reasons or evidence, which are embedded in an individual's total life-experience . . .'[17] However, we need also to recognise that our experience is not neat but it is something, 'which has already been permeated and shaped by various interpretative onlooks'.[18]

There are various kinds of onlooks. For understanding God-talk, it is important to have some understanding of parabolic onlooks (e.g. 'I look on Henry as a brother', 'I look on Smith as a tool' or 'I look on Nazis as vermin'). Here the similarity

69

between what is being compared is said to be 'mainly in terms of an appropriate attitude' toward them.[19] 'I look on X as a Y' comes to mean 'X is *such that* the attitude appropriate to Y is similar to the attitude appropriate to X' where the 'such that' can be filled out upon request. Nazis do not literally have vermin-like qualities and Smith does not literally have tool-like qualities. Henry may or may not have brother-like qualities. All that we are given to understand, when such utterances are uttered, is that there is something about Henry, Smith and the Nazis which makes those attitudes appropriate.

We can, however, with the above examples of parabolic on-look utterances usually spell out what the similarity is. Smith is looked on as a tool because Smith is simply being used to achieve a given end or Smith is thought of as a being devoid of feelings and commitments who simply functions efficiently to achieve whatever task is set for him. But in certain situations it may not be the case that we can so clearly specify what the similarity is. We could say without lapsing into unintelligibility: 'Smith just reminds me of a tool. I can't say why exactly but he does' or we could say: 'My friend Frank tells me that Smith is in fact a tool of the capitalist class and that he is in a position to know, though he can't explain it to me; and I trust Frank.'

We have in God-talk parabolic religious utterances (e.g. 'I look on God as awesomely numinous' or 'I look on God as my moral sovereign' or 'I look on the world as the creature of God'). But there it is very often the case that where a believer employs 'I look on God as Y', (a) he cannot specify the similarity between God and Y, or (b) he trusts the testimony of someone else (for example, Jesus) that God is like Y.[20] More generally what is the case is that we assert there is a likeness but recognise that the likeness is obscure and that we cannot specify what it is. But we do give to understand that the attitude appropriate to Y is appropriate to God. That is, the attitude we have about what is morally sovereign and what is awesomely numinous to us, is also the attitude we have towards God. We are vis-à-vis God like the child whose Father, whom he trusts, tells him 'that the bare wire is very hot'. He understands what a hot thing is and knows enough not to touch hot things, but he doesn't understand electricity and shocks and he has no understanding of how the wire can be hot, but all the same 'hot' serves to inculcate the appropriate attitude. 'The father

70

accommodates his language to the boy's understanding. Later on, the boy will be able to understand language that is literally true. Similarly God accommodates His revelation to human language and understanding, and later on, after death, we will be able to understand in literal terms.'[21]

Evans maintains that for some onlook statements (e.g. 'I look on alcoholism as a disease') 'the meaning of the onlook's content can be ascertained and the legitimacy of the onlook can be debated without reference to attitudes'.[22] This, he claims, can even be true of *some* parabolic onlooks (e.g. 'I look on Henry as a brother'). That is, there can be, if a challenge occurs, a straightforward comparing of X and Y. But religious parabolic utterances of the sort mentioned above 'allow no such direct comparison at all; the comparison between X and Y inherently involves a reference to attitudes'.[23] There the onlook is used to call attention to some (to use Evans' term) 'metaphysical entity' and such parabolic onlooks may be called 'metaphysical'.[24] And with such metaphysical and religious onlooks, the very sincere 'expression of an onlook commits me to a way of behaving and thinking, a mode of life'.[25] I act in accordance with the belief that 'God is like an awesome person but I cannot describe this likeness except by referring to human attitudes'.[26] What God is like in Himself I cannot say, for I can only indirectly describe God.[27]

Evans is perceptive and, it seems to me, on solid ground in arguing that most religious claims are self-involving uses of language. That is to say, in the very making of a religious claim, the claimant, and anyone who accepts the claim, commits himself to acting in a certain way and/or gives to understand that he has an attitude for or against whatever is being claimed. He is also perceptive in arguing that there is a level of understanding in which religious claims require personal conditions for their being fully understood.[28] Understanding religion is bound up with understanding and feeling one's own finitude and moral inadequacy, with having numinous experiences, with having some understanding of selflessness and what it is to care for others and with having a concern to make sense of one's tangled life. It is the having of these experiences that in part constitutes what Evans calls depth-experiences. (I say 'in part' because there are other experiences which count as depth-experiences.) A man who has not had them will have little understanding of God-talk even though he may be able to use God-talk correctly. One could not be deeply religious without profoundly caring about the quality of life; and one would not understand religion unless one understood that such care was essential to it.[29]

However, it is also true, as Evans puts it, that 'there are intelligent men, well-trained men, for whom some or all of the descriptions of depth-experiences have little meaning. Yet one can understand the meaning of talk about "God" only to the extent that one understands talk about the depth-experiences.'[30] But Evans forgets the other side of this coin, the side stressed by MacIntyre and unforgettably and artistically articulated by Dostoevsky, namely that there are men who have these depth-experiences, reflect on them deeply and still find God-talk in one way or another unintelligible or incomprehensible. It isn't that they just interpret their depth-experiences in a different way, but that they cannot understand how the God-talk can be even a *possible* interpretation of such experiences. As I pointed out earlier, Evans confuses a *necessary* with a *sufficient* condition of religious understanding. It is not the case that 'religious language is directly correlated to depth-experiences in its meaning'.[31] Evans rightly rejects a crude reductionism that would maintain that to talk of God is simply a reified way of talking of depth-experiences.[32] But when he says that the 'move from reports of depth-experiences to religious assertions involves an assumption that there exists a hidden divine being, distinct from the world but revealing Himself through the world, a being such that various human attitudes are appropriate responses', he reveals that he is in effect not facing a very crucial question about God-talk, for *it is just the intelligibility of this assumption that is in question, and it is just this question that one hoped his talk of depth-experience would somehow resolve or at least illuminate*. What, to put it crudely, is the difference between asserting and denying the existence of a hidden divine being, distinct from the world, but revealing Himself through the world? There are men, all with similar depth-experiences, who will affirm this religious claim, and there are men who will deny it, and there are also men who will say they can make nothing of it, so that they could decide one way or another. And they all say this while having the same depth-experiences. But then how do they differ except verbally

72

and in their picture preferences, and how is the critic answered who maintains that the difference between them is purely verbal and pictorial? I do not believe there is a good answer to that sceptical question. But if this is so, Evans has not provided us with an answer to the question Smart originally proposed. We are still caught up in the problem of what it could *mean* to claim that 'God sometimes actively reveals Himself in depth-experiences'.[33] If a putative statement really is a genuine statement such that it really has a truth-value, we ought to be able to have some idea of what its truth-value is. But what would it be like to have the slightest inkling as to whether 'God sometimes actively reveals Himself in depth-experiences' is true or false? Until and unless that question can be answered, a sceptical stance vis-à-vis religion seems to be warranted.

III

So our question remains: how are we to, or can we understand the putative truth-claim that there exists a reality transcendent to the world which manifests itself in the world while remaining undetectable in space and time? What would it be like for such an utterance to be either true or false? And what would it be like to specify the objective referent for the terms purporting to characterise such a reality?

Gordon Kaufman in his 'On the Meaning of "God": Transcendence Without Mythology' deals with this problem.[34] The crunch, as he sees it, is how we can make sense of a conception of God where the referent of 'God' is taken to be something objectively real and yet beyond the limits of human experience.[35] Is it the case, he asks, that we can even understand such a conception, make any sense of it at all, or is it the case that what we can understand is limited by the bounds of sense to purely 'this worldly' or 'secular' realities.[36] To make sense of God-talk we must show how it makes sense to speak of something other than that which is in the world.

Kaufman attempts to show how, in purely experiential terms available to utterly 'secular' men, 'God' can be understood as making such a transcendent reference. We need first to ask, Kaufman tells us, what are the experiences in this world which 'seem to require some people to talk' of God.[37] When men seek to understand their own finitude, a concept of God can arise as the reality which is the final limit to their being and power.[38] This, of course, naturally takes a mythological form, but even for men who have cast off 'a two worlds' mythology, there can be a de-mythologised conception of transcendence in which 'the idea of God functions as a limiting concept, i.e. a concept which does not primarily have content in its own right drawn directly out of a specific experience but which refers to that which we do *not* know but which is the ultimate limit of all our experiences'.[39]

Our talk of God as something wholly other 'arises because certain features of experience force us up against the limit(s) of all possible knowledge and experience'.[40] We sense our finitude in being brought up in this way 'against *the Limit of our world*'.[41] It is this that gives us an experiential sense of God and it is this which makes God-talk possible and intelligible. Like Evans, and falling into the same difficulties we found at that point in Evans' analysis, Kaufman points out that those who have not had such experiences or do not reflect on their own finitude will find 'speech about God seeming useless or empty'.[42]

It is in this very talk of 'the Limit' or 'the ultimate Limit' of our world that deep and, I believe, irresolvable difficulties arise for such an account. I will return to this point after I have proceeded a bit with Kaufman's account. It is evident enough, Kaufman points out, that in talk of God more is meant 'than simply the bare and abstract notion of Limit'; but once we abandon anthropomorphic and mythological ways of conceiving of God, it is unclear what more can be meant. Unlike Mavrodes, Kaufman maintains that it is no longer possible, as it once was, to speak with any confidence at all of knowledge of a reality beyond the limits of human experience. If we are really up against *the limits* of our experience and knowledge, then, if limit really means limit, the question arises: is it possible or indeed could it be possible to 'speak of the nature or even the existence of reality beyond those limits?'[43] Is it not nonsense to claim to be able to speak of that which is 'beyond the limits of the humanly experienceable'?[44] Kaufman rightly recognises that it is a self-delusion and indeed 'inconsistent on the one hand to justify talk about God on the ground of our limitedness, and then, on the other, to transcend these limits in order to spell

74

out in some detail the structure of reality that lies beyond them'.[45] But then what kind of conception can we have of 'this notion of ultimate Limit'? Can we even base an intelligible conception on it?

In trying to get a grip on this, we should first note that our experience of finitude is an intellectual–emotional complex. Our experience of radical contingency is not 'an immediate awareness of restriction'.[46] What we do is suffer, see others die, or be born, experience contentment, frustration, disquietude, and the like. But such experiences are not themselves our experience of radical contingency or finitude. Rather, such an experience is a mediated experience arising only when we reflect upon our suffering, frustration, contentment, disquietude, and the like, and try to 'understand ourselves in the light of these happenings'.[47] Our sense of contingency depends on a generalisation from our occasional immediate experiences of limitation. We have that experience when we come to have a distinct onlook, when we come to view ourselves as beings hemmed in on all sides, neither masters of ourselves nor of our world. It is this mediated, reflected experience which is the experiential ground for our conception of God. And, Kaufman avers, with it we are able to interpret certain of our particular immediate experiences, as an experience of our very finitude as human beings. And it is with this conception that the concept of limit needs to be invoked. It is a notion that we metaphorically extend from its original home, where it designates physical boundary lines, to a new context where it designates our sense of being circumscribed or hemmed in. On analogy with a physical boundary, we conceive of 'a limit' as some kind of actual structural reality which limits us. We become aware of actually being limited in our ideas, aptitudes, interests, feelings, training, and the like.

However, there is something which looks at least like a paradox here. We recognise limits in the ordinary case because we have at least some understanding of what it would be like to get beyond them. We can examine a wall or fence and know that there is something beyond it. We can come to be aware of our own class or ethnic origins and the feelings of being more comfortable in certain ways of doing things than in others. We recognise these things as limits because we imaginatively recognise what it would be like to surpass them. God-talk, by contrast, is at home with the notion of an absolute or ultimate Limit. But here we have a very problematical notion indeed – perhaps an *absolute* or *ultimate* Limit is a contradiction in terms – for how could it be a *limit* if it is not, at least in principle, surpassable? Limit, as in a boundary, aptitude or prejudice, implies something limited and determinate to which there is another side, something which in theory, at least, could be surpassed. It looks like 'ultimate limit' or 'absolute limit' – something which cannot even in principle be surpassed – can no more be intelligibly yoked than can 'coloured heat' or 'talkative candy'.

Kaufman, of course, does not agree with this and tries to give sense to 'ultimate limit' by analogy with certain known and well understood relative limits. He grants that the notion of an 'ultimate limit' is the notion (bogus or genuine) of a limit which cannot be surpassed. But he thinks we can work by analogy from the relative limits we do experience to a conception of ultimate limit. That is, we analogically extend the meaning. We move first by analogical extension from our experience of physical boundaries to an uneasy but rather inarticulate awareness of being completely circumscribed and confined. From there we move by the use of models drawn from our particular experiences of being hemmed in to a conception of an ultimate Limit utterly circumscribing us. We gain this conception of an ultimate Limit through the combination of the experiences of *physical limitation, organic limitation* of our powers (failure, exhaustion, illness, weakness, etc.), *personal limitation* (the clash of wills, policies, decisions and purposes) and *normative constraints* such as right/wrong, true/false, good/bad which impinge upon us with categorical demands. It is Kaufman's contention that these are fundamental types of limiting experience which give us models in accordance with which we can come to conceive 'the ultimate Limit'.

Unlike Schleiermacher, Kaufman is *not* saying that we 'have a specific and unique sense of absolute dependence as such' but, what he is claiming is that our various relative dependences, when reflected on together, give us, though in an unavoidably oblique way, some understanding of the ultimate Limit. But we have 'no way of grasping the nature of the ultimate Limit simply and purely in its own terms'. Indeed, in our very conception of an ultimate Limit we have something of which it

76

would not even make sense to say that we had directly apprehended its character. If, however, it is a Limit beyond which
we could never move at all, then trivially there can be no direct
experience of it. But, Kaufman continues, 'the ultimate Limit—
being that which is apprehended as the *real* and *effective* restriction on our being and movement (no mere "empty idea")
– is grasped as concrete actuality impinging on us, i.e. not
merely abstractedly but as having some concrete character or
nature'.[48]

Kaufman summarises the way in which the notion of the
ultimate Limit is formulated and, in the very formulating of it,
he discloses its inadequacy. He schematises it in five stages:

(1) There must be particular concrete experiences of limitation of the several types described.

(2) The self must be sufficiently mature and reflective to be
able to move from consciousness of these particular
experiences to a more general concept of limitation or
finitude.

(3) We must become aware of the significance of the fact
that each of us, as individual persons, is inescapably
hemmed in, limited; and this unblinkered awareness
must arise together with powerful emotions which con-
tribute to our sense of finitude.

(4) This awareness of my own radical contingency may then
give rise to the question of *what* it is which so confines and
limits me.

(5) The ultimate Limit may then be conceived in terms of
one (or possibly some combination) of the four types of
finite limiter.[49]

After setting out those stages, Kaufman remarks, puzzlingly,
'it is certainly conceivable that we are limited ultimately by
some (one) reality'. If we can rightly assume that the notion of
an ultimate Limit' is an intelligible one, then this may be so,
but that we can justifiably make that assumption is just what is
at issue here. It is just this that Kaufman is trying to establish!
And it is just to such a notion that we leap when we move from
step four to step five. Note that in the first four steps there are
no problematic conceptions – metaphysical notions that might
prove a scandal to the intellect. However, with (5) we have the
notion of an 'ultimate Limit' introduced and this is just our

troubling notion. It is not, as Kaufman remarks, just that 'there seems to be no compelling necessity to move from step (3) in the above process through (4) and (5)'. That would be tolerable enough since, if that were so, we would remain with the choice of either interpreting our direct depth-experiences as giving us a sense of finitude in terms of the four types of finite limiter experienced when we reflect on what limits us, or alternatively we could look on our experiences as attesting to the fact that what limits us is some one reality beyond and behind these finite limiters, namely the ultimate Limiter. But here Kaufman is pulling himself up by his own bootstraps, for it is precisely the very idea of there being some 'one reality beyond and behind these finite limiters' that we are trying to find a footing for, trying to find out what, if anything, it means. The question, as he himself insists, is one of *meaning* and not of *truth*, but where the going gets tough, Kaufman simply uses and does not elucidate these opaque notions. We need to understand what, if anything, could count as an 'ultimate Limiter' or as 'an absolute Limit'.

However, it is just at this point where Kaufman does not help us at all. He tells us that all our knowledge is rooted in 'experiences of the finite', that the ultimate Limiter is not and cannot be directly apprehended and that we do not have a specific and unique sense of absolute dependence. What we have experienced are physical, organic, personal, and normative limitations. But how are we to understand what it would be like to interpret or look on these limitations as mediators of the *ultimate Limiter*? We understand the four concrete kinds of limitations – all limitations in a perfectly straightforward and unproblematical sense – but how, through understanding those limitations and indeed from dwelling on and taking to heart that we are so limited, are we to apprehend 'the ultimate Limit' as the real and effective restriction of our being and movement? Isn't this as unintelligible as being asked to view Tuesday as talkative or music as mountainous? We do not know what we have to do to make such an interpretation, to give such a reading to our experiences. We indeed, as I pointed out in discussing Smart and Evans, could have depth-experiences or numinous experiences and be quite vividly aware of our finitude and radical contingency and yet we could perfectly well be without a clue as to what this talk of an ultimate

Limiter or absolute limitation was about, except as a compendious way of talking about the various particular kinds of 'relative limitations' together. But, if this is all that is being said, then we have not managed to say anything of religious significance. To continue, if this is our understanding of what is involved, to speak of 'relative limits' and 'an absolute limit' is at best misleading. But it is evident enough that Kaufman wants to say more than this.

Perhaps we come closer to gaining a grasp of 'the ultimate Limit' if we work with the analogy of a finite personal limiter. Kaufman claims it is the model to use in order to conceive of the ultimate Limit as mediating the God of the Judeo-Christian tradition.[50] As Kaufman puts it himself, 'talk about God appears when the ultimate Limit is understood on analogy with the experience of *personal limiting* as known in the intercourse and interaction of personal wills'.[51] This conceiving of God in quasi-personal terms fits in well with the biblical God and it helps to give us an experiential sense of what is involved in transcendence. After all, human beings in their innermost being remain inaccessible to others except as they choose to show their feelings and thoughts in their words and deeds.[52] One might, though this is a slightly inflated idiom, speak of the transcendence of the self. Indeed, Kaufman is willing to work with a notion 'of a self whose active center is *beyond* that which is directly experienced' and who reveals himself to others. By working with this personalistic model, we not only can say something about the ultimate limit but we can see how we can obliquely refer to what is beyond it.[53] Finite selves can have thoughts and feelings not directly accessible to me (or anyone else) and can at their choosing convey their thoughts and feelings to me and so, hidden from me, remain transcendent to me. By analogy, we can interpret the ultimate limit in quasi-personal terms as a transcendent Self or as mediating a transcendent Self not directly accessible to me, who can, if He chooses, reveal Himself to me or remain hidden and incomprehensible to me, and thus transcendent to me.[54]

Even when we consider human beings, we need to remember, Kaufman contends, that we can never directly experience another; all an individual directly experiences are the external physical sights and sounds which a person makes, not 'the deciding, acting, purposing center of the self – though I have

79

no doubts these externalities are not *merely* physical phenomena but are the outward and visible expression of inner thought, purpose and intention'.[55] In relations with other people, 'I presuppose a reality (the active center of the self) *beyond* that which I immediately perceive . . .'[56] In speaking, in using our common language, this reality reveals itself to me as something more than merely a physical being. Here we have an understanding, with a purely finite reality, of what it is to have 'an awareness of genuine activity and reality beyond and behind what is directly open to our view'.

By analogy with the finite self, God should be viewed as a hidden personal reality who 'cannot be identified with what is accessible to or within our experience, not even with the ultimate Limit of our experience; rather this Limit must be grasped as the medium through which God encounters us'.[57] Recall that religious experience is, most centrally, revelation, i.e. God's self-manifestation or disclosure. Working with this analogy, God Himself should be conceived 'as the dynamic acting reality beyond the limit' who, as He wills, manifests Himself to us.[58] So we have, as long as we stick with this model, some conception of the nature of reality beyond the limit. (There is no understanding of 'God' without some model, for there is no direct apprehension of God.) However, there remains the problem about the very notion of 'the ultimate Limit', for Kaufman would have it that the nature of God is only 'known through the mediation of the ultimate Limit'.[59] But if the notion of 'the ultimate Limit' is unintelligible, then there can be no understanding of God. Yet, it is this very notion which appears at least to be unintelligible.

Let us, however, now set this last consideration aside, and work with Kaufman's analogy. First, we should ask if he is right about the finite self. Is the essentially Cartesian picture he gives us of human beings an intelligible, one? (In asking this, I am not asking whether it is the most adequate conceptualisation of man but I am asking whether it is indeed even an intelligible conception of man. It seems to be at first blush, but when we probe it, as Ryle, Wittgenstein, Strawson, Hampshire and Williams have probed it in various ways, does it really turn out to be intelligible?[60]) For Kaufman, 'A self in its active center is never directly open to view, but is known only as he reveals himself in communication and communion.'[61] Presumably this is some kind of conceptual remark and not something that just in fact happens to be so. Unlike the situation of an illusive warbler high in a tree which one hears but does not see, it is not just that we do not catch a glimpse of the self – 'the inner man' – but that we cannot because 'the self' is the *kind* of reality that cannot be seen. (Perhaps Kaufman does not want to say that, but, if he does not, then, like the man trying to spy out the illusive beautifully singing warbler, we just have not looked carefully enough yet: the self is not an *essentially* hidden or another kind of reality distinct from mundane realities and thus we have no model for understanding 'God'.)

However, in talking about a human being as essentially a self, which in its active centre is never directly open to view, we, at the very least, make the concept of a human being far more problematical than it is. Surely the empirical facts to which Kaufman alludes do not require such a conception of 'the self'. We indeed have thoughts and feelings which we choose not to reveal and we are often illusive and mysterious to each other. And there is a sense in which each of us has a certain privileged access to his own thoughts and feelings. But even this is a more relative matter than Kaufman gives us to understand, for sometimes in our behaviour and words we show thoughts, feelings and attitudes that we are not aware of but that a psychiatrist, friend, or shrewd enemy can spy out. Our privileged access is not absolute, but even if it were, this need not conjure up a Cartesian picture of 'the inner man'. As Strawson has shown, a person is not two distinct realities, a body and a mind, as a peach has flesh and a pit.[62] We cannot look intelligibly on a person as just a body or as just a mind or as part body and part mind. A person is a complex being who has thoughts and feelings but is not an illusive self with an 'active center never directly open to view'. 'I never directly experience another' is a deviant utterance but, given a reasonable construal of what might be meant by it, it is false, as anyone knows who has been deeply involved with another or who has even walked arm in arm with another through a long spring day. There is no need to invoke that dualistic picture to represent and interpret the facts to which Kaufman alludes.

Be that as it may, may we not so interpret them if we choose? People have repeatedly tried to do so and many are convinced that we can. And, if we try to interpret the facts in this way, the self becomes very mysterious indeed; indeed, it is true that such a concept of the self is without doubt very problematical. But how could it be anything else, since it is the notion of a self which is some 'logically private sort of thing' that cannot even in principle be observed or empirically and inter-subjectively detected? This is, indeed, a very problematic notion. If this is our model for understanding God, we are giving sense to the obscure by appealing to the obscure.

To the retort that God is a mystery and thus we cannot expect clarity here, it should in turn be replied that the concept of such a self is so problematical, so near to being meaningless, if indeed not meaningless, that we are not justified in being confident that we have in it an intelligible model for under-standing God. It is not just obscurity but obscurity rooted in what may well be, and most likely is, unintelligibility that is at issue.

However, let us also put these issues to the side and assume that such a dualism is both intelligible and true. I want to say that even so, it is not evident that Kaufman has shown us how we can make sense out of non-anthropomorphic God-talk. Has such talk of 'a self' that is never directly observed or even observable by others, given us a model for a conception of a God which is not an embodied self, as the finite self is; and does it provide a model for 'a self' transcendent to the world? We know, for example, how to identify an embodied self – a Hans, Bill or Jane – but not how to identify a 'non-embodied self', some kind of 'pure spirit'. We know what it is for Hans to act, to do something, but we have no understanding of what it would be like for a Pure Spirit to do something or fail to do something.[63] With an embodied self, 'whose active center is never directly open to view', we have (we are now assuming) an understanding of 'transcendence' in the sense that we under-stand what it means to speak of there being something not directly open to view. But this gives us no footing at all in our attempt to gain some understanding of what it would mean to speak of a reality transcendent to the world. For these hidden realities are always associated with discrete, determinate reali-ties acting in the world. The universe, by contrast, is not a discrete thing or entity of which it would make sense to say that there were hidden realities or a reality beyond it or behind it. But the concept of God Kaufman wants to make intelligible

82

is the concept of 'a being transcending our world'.[64] He is not always consistent here, for at one point he identifies God with 'the reality which ultimately limits us on all sides', allowing, by that characterisation, God to be identified with the world as reductive materialists conceive of it. But this is not the usual thrust of his essay, for there God is taken to be the reality which lies beyond the limit.[65] Thus, even if we assume the truth and the intelligibility of dualism, it is still very questionable whether Kaufman has given us a model which will enable us to see how non-anthropomorphic God-talk can be intelligible.

More generally and going back to Kaufman's starting point, it is fair to say that it is his very mode of speech that pushes us unnecessarily in the direction of this obscure talk of 'an ultimate Limiter'. Note the following perfectly natural and unproblematic way to talk about what Kaufman, like Smart and Evans, takes to be his experiential base for talk of God. We note the birth, suffering, alienation and death of others. We ourselves alternatively suffer and experience moments of peace and happiness. We feel constrained, hemmed in, inadequate and bound to act in certain ways and we experience the conflict of the wills and wishes of other people. And when we reflect on these matters, and matters like them, we find that there are objective conditions, physical, organic, psychological, moral and inter-personal, which limit us. That is to say, these are the things that hem us in or constrain us in certain ways. I am confident that in a fuller picture of the limiting conditions – a picture which gives us a fuller sense of how we are beings with limited capacities – we would have to say other things as well, but they would remain things of that same secular sort. That is to say, we would have more of the same kind of thing. But there is no need at all in accounting for those experiences and in accounting for their limiting conditions to the full to invoke such a problematic notion as an 'ultimate Limit'. That is just gratuitously brought in by Kaufman. It is not even a case of a choice, representing different metaphysical perspectives, of how to interpret experience. What we have is a case of a way of accounting for these experiences which is unproblematic and another alleged 'interpretation' which is so obscure that it is not clear that it even counts as an interpretation.

By introducing a certain way of talking about being brought up by certain experiences against 'the limits of our world' or by talking of certain features of experience forcing us 'up against the limit(s) of all possible knowledge and experience', we get, by the very vocabulary we adopt, into the position of trying to struggle to articulate some obscure notion of 'an ultimate Limit'. For some people our talk here can be powerfully emotive; but all the same it is very indeterminate. What we should conclude is that it is the *manner* and not the *matter* that drives us to talk about 'boundary situations' and/or into utilising God-talk, or at least profound *sounding* metaphysical talk, to talk of some 'ultimate Limit' which accounts for our sense of finitude and moral inadequacy. But there is no need to adopt that mode of speech to make sense of our depth-experiences and even if we try to so interpret them, our key concepts in such an interpretation are so problematic that it is not known if we have said anything that could possibly be either true or false.

The problem we started with is the problem of how we could give experiential sense to God-talk which makes a putatively transcendent reference so that we could show how such religious claims are genuine truth-claims. But toward this end, Kaufman's analysis, subtle and complex as it is, has been no more help than Smart's or Evans'. Kaufman wanted to exhibit 'the experiential basis for – and thus the root meaning of – the word "God"', but he has failed on several counts, including (and very fundamentally) his attempt to make sense of the notion of 'an ultimate Limit'. And in not pulling this off, he has failed (a) to indicate what could count as an objective referent for 'God' and (b) to show how we can utilise this word in a religiously appropriate way to make either true or false statements.[66]

IV

Ian T. Ramsey also attempts to display cogently what he takes to be the experiential basis of God-talk.[67] Like Kaufman, he agrees that unless talk of God has such an experiential basis, it will be empty and pointless and will convey very little to us; and he too tries to exhibit how it can be the case that there are genuine religious truth-claims and how it is that 'God' has an objective referent appropriate to the religious expectations of the faithful. But his attempt at a perspicuous representation

84

takes a different turn. The stress is on the necessity for having models grounded in situations of 'cosmic disclosure'. The key problem of reference, as he calls it, gets discussed against this background.

'Belief in God', Ramsey contends, 'arises from what I have called cosmic disclosures, situations where the Universe "comes alive", where a "dead", "dull", "flat" existence takes on "depth" or another "dimension".'[68] There is a wide variety of situations under which such a disclosure can occur. It can come from the reading of the Bible, from seeing a family together or two lovers walking hand in hand, from listening to Palestrina or from standing on a mountain peak and seeing range after range of mountains opening up to view.[69] Such disclosures are cosmic 'because of their all embracing range', because with them 'the whole Universe confronts us'. A paradigm case of such a disclosure is given by Ramsey:

> ... we are walking in a remote, mountainous country and as night comes on we are filled with all kinds of uncertainties and anxieties. But then we refresh ourselves at a mountain stream, look up to the stars as symbols of stability, and find our path illumined by the moon. A sense of kinship with nature strikes us; the Universe is reliable after all.[70]

However, in talking about what happens when such a disclosure occurs, Ramsey says something which seems to me very strange, radically unclear, and not at all to be something we actually have or even understand as something we might come to have from having the experiences Ramsey characterises. Ramsey says that when we are so confronted by the universe 'we are entitled to speak of there being a single individuation expressing itself in each and all of these disclosures'.[71] But what, if anything, is meant in such a context by 'a single individuation' is thoroughly unclear. Ramsey tells us, as if this were an elucidation, 'from any and every cosmic disclosure we can claim to believe in one X (where X for the moment remains to be elucidated) precisely because we talk of there being "one world"'.[72] But this is elucidating the obscure with the equally obscure. Except in a way in which it is otiose so to speak, why should we talk, after having such a disclosure, of the world being 'one world' and even if we were to talk that way, why, because of this recognition of 'there being "one world"', should we say that we believe in one X or believe in a 'single individuation'? No reason is given by Ramsey or even suggested and none suggests itself. Yet these disclosures are said to be 'ontologically privileged' in the sense that 'they disclose that which confronts us as a basic "given"'.[73]

It is clear enough that this given is like Kaufman's conception of limit in that it is 'that which is set over against ourselves in every situation of this kind'.[74] But when Ramsey goes on to say that in doing this it 'individuates the universe', we have another incredible obscurity, for we have no idea at all what counts as 'individuating the Universe' or 'failing to individuate the Universe'. No coherent use or indeed no use at all has been specified here. The engine is plainly idling. We have a term of art with no directions for use. (The same thing also obtains when he speaks, also without explanation, a few sentences later of 'the whole Universe being particularised'.) Presumably the objective referent of such a disclosure is that which we are aware of as confronting us as that which is set over against ourselves in every situation and as that which 'individuates the universe', though, since we do not understand what is meant by 'individuating the universe', such talk has little communication value.

But even assuming we can overcome these hurdles, why should we (or should we) talk 'of the objective reference of a cosmic disclosure in terms of God'? When we talk about God and link this talk with that which occurs in disclosure situations, there is an extensive use of images, metaphors and models. In the Bible, God is modelled on 'father, mother, nurse, brother, husband, friend, warrior, shepherd, farmer, metalworker, builder, potter, fuller, physician, judge, tradesman, King, fisherman, and scribe'.[75] 'Ye are my sheep, the sheep of my pasture are many . . .' (Ezek. 34:31), 'The Lord is the true God . . . and an everlasting King' (Jer. 10:7), and 'The Lord is our judge, the Lord is our lawgiver' (Isa. 33:22). Some models, Ramsey maintains, are more adequate than others but it is not possible to dispense with models altogether and understand what we are talking about independently of the model. What we need, to get anything approaching a reasonable representation of God, is to use many models and fertile models. To get a belief in God from a cosmic disclosure, we must have some characterisation of God in accordance with some model.

86

Our key problem, according to Ramsey, is 'how, with this account of models and disclosures, can we be sure we are talking about God, and not merely about ourselves or, as it is sometimes expressed, about "our own experience" '.[76] Ramsey maintains that the only way in which it is possible to test whether one has had a cosmic disclosure, is by reference to a model, for without the model 'there is no sensible articulation' of the alleged cosmic disclosure.[77] 'A theological model is a way of understanding what has been objectively disclosed in a cosmic disclosure.'[78]

But how can we tell, even in principle, that these models are models of God? The first thing to note, Ramsey tells us – surprisingly, as if earlier he had prepared the ground for the question – is that 'there is only *one* reference for *all* disclosure illustrations, it is this which, in ways better or worse, *every* model contrives to talk about'.[79] There seems to be, as far as I can see, no reason to believe that this is so nor is it at all evident that Ramsey has even given us a *supposed* reason for believing this to be so. Perhaps his obscure remarks about 'a single individuation' or 'individuating the Universe' are meant to justify or explicate this claim. But it is difficult to see how such vapid notions could justify or explicate anything.

There is a further feature of theological models that, I believe, compounds these difficulties. Such models, unlike picturing models, are such that the objective reference of what the model is a model of is never given and never can be given independently of the model. But we need to ask whether this is an intelligible conception of a model. For if X is a model, must it not in principle at least be possible to say what X is a model of? If we cannot, not just because we have not tried hard enough, but because, as with 'theological models', we are *logically* barred from doing so, we do not have something we can recognise as distinct from X which X models. Ramsey aptly puts the crucial difficulty concerning his talk of models as follows, but does not succeed, as far as I can see, in showing how his account escapes these difficulties.

To use the concept of model, it might be said, presupposes, an original with which the model may be compared. Must not this whole talk of models therefore presuppose some knowledge of God which is quite independent of models and against which the success (or failure) of a particular symbol or model can be measured?[80]

But Ramsay, for reasons similar to those given by Evans and Kaufman, denies that there can be any knowledge of God which is independent of models. Rather, Ramsey believes that the difficulty is answered by recognising that models are of different types and that the above considerations only apply to picturing models but not to 'theological models', for they are disclosure-models – models which do not picture.

However, it does not seem to me that this argument meets the point at issue, for it is not that all models must picture their originals but that all models, like all metaphors, must be models of something in order to be models. But if there is no way, even in principle, to describe a difference between the model and what it is supposedly a model of, there is no way of distinguishing them so that we can distinguish the model from what it models. Surely this must be true of any kind of model if the word 'model' is to have any sense. What seems to be the case is that we have a lot of anthropomorphic conceptions – father, love, shepherd, potter, King, lawgiver – which we do not want to apply literally to God for fear of making Him Zeus-like. But these are the only ways we have of talking about God which are sufficiently concrete and related to our experience not to be utterly problematical. But even with a multiple use of such anthropomorphic terms, we still have only these terms and the anthropomorphic realities they characterise. They do not help us to make a reference beyond that which is at least in principle experienceable. Ramsey shows us how our concept of God can remain anthropomorphic and intelligible but not, as he wishes, non-anthropomorphic and intelligible.

5 Rondo with Concluding Variations

I

This essay has been an articulation and a defence of scepticism. The core of it has been devoted to showing that non-anthropomorphic conceptions of God do not make sense, that we have no sound grounds for believing that the central truth-claims of Christianity are genuine truth-claims and that we have no sound grounds for believing that there is a religiously viable concept of God which is sufficiently intelligible to make Jewish, Christian or Islamic belief justifiable or even acceptable *de fide*. In fact, the evidence we do have justifies the claim that such God-talk and such putative beliefs are incoherent.

If this claim is justified and no anthropomorphic conception of God is religiously viable, then we are also plainly justified in giving a sceptical and negative response to the logically posterior sceptical questions concerning the truth-claims of religion. That is to say, we have good reasons for believing not only that those religious doctrines are not true but also that they *cannot* be true. And since Judaism, Christianity and Islam purport to give us central truths about the universe and man's nature and destiny, it cannot be reasonable, if my above sceptical arguments are correct, to remain or become a Jew, Christian or Moslem. Such religious beliefs should definitely be rejected.

There are sceptics (Hansen, Hook, Matson, Nagel, Scriven, to take some outstanding examples) who do not believe that *such* sceptical arguments are justified.[1] They think that the central strands of Jewish, Christian and Islamic religious discourse make sense and that we indeed know well enough what it would be like for there to be a God and what would have to be the case for 'God created man', 'God protects us all', and indeed even 'God exists' to be true. It is not, they maintain, the coherence of such talk that generally should be at issue, but the truth of such religious claims. Their grounds for scepticism turn on their arguments concerning what they take to be the extremely low order of probability or the groundlessness of religious beliefs. They attempt to show that the likelihood of such religious beliefs being true is very inconsiderable indeed. The claim is that these central religious beliefs are intelligible but groundless and that therefore we should not believe them.

However, it is my belief that the conflict between these two kinds of scepticism is more apparent than real. The concept of God that these sceptics (Hanson, Hook, Matson, etc.) *show* to be intelligible is a belief in an anthropomorphic God and as I indicated in Chapter One, such a Zeus-like conception is indeed intelligible. But it is not such a concept that is said to be without sense by sceptics of the stripe we have been examining. Rather they have argued that such anthropomorphic religious conceptions are recognisably idolatrous, and they certainly would agree that there is no good reason to believe that such realities exist. It is the more religiously attractive non-anthropomorphic beliefs – beliefs which religiously reflective people are increasingly driven to – which turn out on inspection to be incoherent. They are used in putative assertions to make allegedly synthetic factual claims but in actuality these claims are without genuine truth-value, for we have no idea what their truth-value is or how even in principle we could go about ascertaining their truth-value. One type of sceptic argues that religious beliefs are beliefs in an anthropomorphic deity and that in fact these beliefs are false beliefs; the other type of sceptic speaks, as well, of a confused notion of a non-anthropomorphic deity and argues that such a belief is incoherent. Plainly there is no direct conflict here.

That this is so comes out interestingly in an essay by N. R. Hanson. Hanson remarks:

'God exists' could in principle be established for all factually – it just happens not to be, certainly not for everyone! Suppose, however, that on next Tuesday morning, just after our breakfast, all of us in this one world are knocked to our knees by a percussive and ear-shattering thunderclap. Snow swirls; leaves drop from trees; the earth heaves and buckles; buildings topple and towers tumble; the sky is ablaze with an eerie, silvery light. Just then, as all the people of this world

90

look up, the heavens open – the clouds pull apart – revealing an unbelievably immense and radiant Zeus-like figure, towering up above us like a hundred Everests. He frowns darkly as lightning plays across the features of his Michael-angeloid face. He then points down – at me! – and exclaims, for every man, woman, and child to hear: 'I have had quite enough of your too-clever logic-chopping and word-watching in matters of theology. Be assured, N. R. Hanson, that I do most certainly exist.'

Nor is this to be conceived of as a private transaction between the ultimate Divinity and myself – for everyone in the world witnessed, 'knew by acquaintance', what had transpired between the heavens and myself, and all men heard what was entoned to me from on high. T.V. cameras and audio-tapes also recorded this event for all posterity.

Please do not dismiss this example as a playful, irreverent Disney-oid contrivance. The conceptual point here is that *if* such a remarkable event were to transpire, *I* for one should certainly be convinced that God does exist. That matter of fact would have been settled once and for all time.[2]

Surely, those sceptics, who wish to establish the truth-value of God-talk only to go on to establish, as Hanson ably does, the evident falsity and absurdity of such religious beliefs, have made their case that *such* a conception of God is coherent. We know what it would be like for such a reality to exist and we know that there is no such reality. Such a sceptic, in short, has met the falsification challenge head on; he has described a conceivable state of affairs, an empirically determinate state of affairs, such that if such a state of affairs were to obtain, it would be reasonable to assert that such a Zeus-like God exists. (Paul Feyerabend in an essay in the same volume as Hanson's gives a powerful argument to establish that even then we would not *have* to say that such a being exists.[3]) Such a figure, such a god, is indeed conceivable and is not conceptually problematic. But, of course, there is no such being. Moreover, what is quite crucial to note here is that almost all believers are of the opinion that such a god is a *deus ex machina*, a Zeusoid conception, that they do not accept and do not take to be something one has any grounds at all for believing to exist. Indeed, religiously sensitive and conceptually astute believers would add that if

91

such a supernatural being were to exist, it would be religiously anomalous, for such a reality is surely not evidently a reality supremely worthy of worship. The central thing to recognise in this context is that such a conception of God, though perfectly intelligible, is in effect a Mickey Mouse god and not the God of religiously and conceptually sensitive Jews and Christians. (If someone says: 'Well then let us forget about being religiously and conceptually sensitive and preserve intelligibility', then one pays the price, as Hanson, Matson and others show, of having a religious belief which is absurdly false – little better than a gross superstition.) 'God', as Father Copleston has put it, 'is described in such a way that he cannot be perceived, and that anything which can be perceived is not a Deity.'[4] The conception of God in Judeo-Christian discourses, Copleston stresses, is that of a 'purely spiritual being' and hence it is not even the *kind* of being that Hanson describes. Hanson has got the matter all wrong. The Judeo-Christian God, unlike Zeus and Apollo, is not the kind of reality that is even 'perceptible in principle'. MacIntyre, sceptic that he is, drives home a point very much like Father Copleston's. Judaism and Christianity, MacIntyre argues, are quite distinct 'from all those pretheistic beliefs in which sacredness inheres in features of nature and society. The gods of the heathen are partially visible; the God of Abraham is wholly invisible.'[5] Hanson's god, and the god of the other anthropomorphic sceptics, is *not* the God of developed Christianity but a heathen god. Such god-talk is perfectly verifiable, but, by contrast, God-talk for Christians and Jews is not a talk that makes such evidently verifiable statements of fact.

'God is not perceptible even in principle' is what Wittgenstein would call a grammatical remark. Thus the Hanson-type sceptic has not succeeded in talking about the God of Judaism and Christianity and showing that such religious claims make verifiable statements of fact. And other such sceptics (Hook, for example) who do not explicitly assume, as Hanson does, that God is at least in principle observable, make assumptions about the logic of God-talk which presuppose that God is at least in principle visible or in some other way empirically observable or detectable.[6] Yet this is just the sort of reality that God is not. But where, as for Hugo Meynell and Ninian Smart, God is not so anthropomorphised yet putative God-statements (e.g. 'God protects His creation') are taken to be confirmable or infirmable, we still have no idea at all what would even in principle confirm or infirm them such that we could exhibit the difference in truth-value between 'God protects His creation' and 'There is no one transcendent reality which protects finite creatures'. Both putative statements seem at least to be equally compatible with any and every actual or conceivable empirically identifiable state of affairs.[7] But this means that, for such utterances, we cannot determine their truth-value. They purport to have a truth-value but we cannot say what their truth-value is. It would appear that this is the fate of all religiously central strands of non-anthropomorphic God-talk.

However, even if the last part of my above claim is too strong because of the possibility that the same evidence might be used to confirm or infirm incompatible hypotheses, the basic difficulty remains that we have not, as Peirce observed, been able to do more than *verbally* distinguish between the religious claim and the sceptical claim. There is no verifiable (empirical or experiential) difference between them so that we can have some understanding of what non-verbal difference there is between what the Christian asserts and the sceptic denies. Choice of terminology apart, we want to know the difference between their respective putative assertions.

It is just such a sceptical point that Christian philosophical theologians I discussed in Chapters Three and Four were trying to overcome. I have tried to establish that their efforts come to naught and the sceptical question still remains with us. But it is a sceptical question in terms of the coherence of the discourse in question: it is not a Hanson-type scepticism which takes the claims in question as evidently intelligible but just in fact false. The latter type scepticism falls foul of the objection that it is question-begging, for it requires, illegitimately and mistakenly, that God be construed as a material object or a reality very like a material object open to the kinds of empirical standards of confirmation and disconfirmation that are appropriate to such objects. But God is not *that kind* of reality. That is to say, that is not how God is conceived in the more developed forms of Judaism or Christianity. And therefore such sceptical criticisms are unjustified. But the kind of scepticism examined and developed in this essay does not fall prey to such objections. It instead points out that such God-talk purports to make truth-claims but that we have no idea at all how we can determine or even go about trying to determine whether such putative statements are true or probably true or false or probably false. But it is no good saying they have truth-value if we cannot, as it appears at least we cannot, say *what* their truth-value is; and it is no good claiming, as does E. L. Mascall in his Gifford Lectures, that, all the same, we understand such utterances even if we have no idea of how we could distinguish between a true claim and a false claim in this domain.[8]

II

There are sceptics who remain sceptical of my claims and claims like them about the incoherence or unintelligibility of God-talk. They are, for their liking, too close to discredited positivist talk about such discourse being meaningless or cognitively meaningless. We can indeed sometimes understand a statement without being able to specify the confirming or disconfirming conditions of that statement and, it will be claimed by some, we can even sometimes understand a statement (putative statement) without having any understanding at all of what could even in principle count as confirming or infirming conditions of that statement (putative statement). Such philosophers conclude that while the kind of challenge about truth-conditions pressed in this essay do not show the unintelligibility or incoherence of such religious claims, it does in effect rightly challenge the rational tenability of such conceptions.[9] What it really shows, on such an account, is that if someone makes a religious claim and yet has no idea at all what will count for or against its truth, then that person is making a claim that is without rational warrant. Moreover, to make such a claim self-consciously under such conditions is to make a claim which is indeed irrational. If a truth-claim is utterly unverifiable, we can have no grounds for making it or holding it. We must not make the mistake of Wittgensteinian Fideists such as Phillips and Holmer and assume that to show that religious utterances are intelligible or even self-consistent is necessarily to show they have sufficient rational warrant to be justified or even reasonable. Religious utterances may be intelligible but all the same irrational.[10]

94

This kind of sceptical argument contrasts both with the central sceptical arguments pursued in this essay and the Hanson type scepticism which simply argues for the falsity of the claims of religion. It is an important argument that deserves more consideration than it has received and it will be particularly crucial in the debate between belief and scepticism, if the kind of sceptical arguments I have deployed about the coherence of God-talk turn out to be mistaken.

However, as it stands, it is surely open to counter-arguments by Wittgensteinian Fideists. Such a sceptic must at least meet the following counter-claims readily utilisable in counter-arguments: (a) there are, aside from some purely formal criteria, no transfield criteria for rationality; (b) beliefs which are crucial to make sense of one's life and which are not in conflict with claims for which we do have evidence, may reasonably be believed even though they are beliefs for which we have no evidence; (c) faith is essential to religious belief, to have faith is to take on trust that for which there is no good evidence and this can be reasonably done when what one takes on faith is not contrary to the evidence.[11]

I do not mean to suggest that such a sceptic could not in turn counter such Fideistic arguments, but I do mean to give to understand that such a counter has yet to be carefully and convincingly made by such a sceptic. But be that as it may, the form of scepticism I have defended does not (if its central thrust is correct) need to pursue these questions, for it undermines the very assumptions made by such a Fideist.

It is natural to respond here by claiming that my sceptical account also makes assumptions which are themselves question-begging vis-à-vis the believer. It will be maintained that like the Hanson type sceptic, I am in effect still assuming that the reality of God is somehow like the reality of the Milky Way, that God is somehow some wondrous kind of object, that existence claims about God in order to be genuine existence claims are to be treated as a sub-class of experientially confirmable or infirmable claims.

The qualification 'in effect' is crucial here, for I have been at pains to deny that God, where we are not being anthropomorphic, is conceived of as being any kind of object. But what is intended here in this anticipated criticism of my account is the claim I am in effect hoodwinking myself. That is to say,

95

the pattern of my sceptical argument implicitly makes assumptions which, when clearly brought to mind, I hasten to reject, but then when I am not thinking about them the old picture reasserts itself. As Rush Rhees would put it, what I am unwittingly doing half the time, when it is crucial to my argument, is to construe 'I believe in God' as if it were parallel to 'I believe in the existence of a nebula beyond any we have observed'.[12] But this is plainly a mistake. We must recognise that 'God is not an object', like 'The world is not an object', is in Wittgenstein's sense a grammatical remark comparable to 'A husband is not a woman' or 'A priest is not a layman'. If we keep this grammatical remark concerning religious discourse firmly before our minds, we will not make the mistaken assumptions I made or mistakenly ask, as I have and as Flew has, '*What* is this God that "God" denotes?' We must get out from under the assumption that the language of Christianity is to be construed as a language which describes matters of fact, albeit extraordinary matters of fact. It is absurd to think that we could carry out some 'kind of investigation to *find out* what God is . . .'[13] We do not learn the meaning of the word 'God' by having someone point and say 'That is God'. But I am still in effect assuming that 'God' is a kind of substantive that could be taught in that way.

It is not that in talking about God our language does not refer to anything, but that 'talking about' here has a very different employment than in talking about the London Bridge, the Milky Way or even about the Omega Minus. 'God' is unique by virtue of the fact that the universe, taken as a single spatially all-inclusive reality, is the only basis for identifying God as a single individuation. It makes no sense to talk about trying to locate God, as one might locate the Milky Way or the Omega Minus, for it makes no sense to talk of locating the universe.[14] 'God' could not fail to have a referent as 'red mail box' or 'Tom Jones' might fail to have a referent; 'God' cannot fail to have a referent because there could be no problem about locating the universe. The scope of observables through which God is disclosed is all-inclusive, i.e. it is the universe, though not only the universe, that 'God' refers to rather than to a particular object or cluster of particular objects. Moreover, it is due to that very distinctive feature of the reference range of 'God', that (a) the falsification challenge is not to the point (since 'God' refers to

96

everything, we could not say what must be the case for God *not* to exist), (b) it makes no sense to try to locate God, and (c) there is no possibility that 'God' might have no referent, since there plainly is a universe. I fail, so the complaint goes, to take proper note of these things and thus I end up making sceptical pseudo-problems, failing in essence to note the idiosyncratic and unique employments of 'God'.

Concerning these Wittgensteinian moves, I should like to say several things. Firstly, they seem to commit such a Wittgensteinian theologian to the claim that if the universe exists, God exists. That is hardly a grammatical remark, but if we construe it, as we should, as some kind of contingent statement, it should also be noted that it is a claim for which no evidence has been given, and indeed, it is not even evident what would or even could count as evidence for or against it. If instead, like Plantinga, we, by what is in effect a stipulation, construe it as a grammatical remark, we should (*a*) recognise the arbitrariness of this and (*b*) recognise that *by definition* this makes the universe a dependent entity, but clearly that is something we cannot do *by definition*, even if it does make sense to talk in that way. Whether something depends on something else depends finally on how things are and not on how we choose to talk. Secondly, if 'God' refers to something more than the universe, as well as the universe, no coherent account has been given of this 'more'. 'God is the universe and more' is a deviant utterance. If someone claims to understand it, he needs to make plain what it means and what reasons he has for thinking it true. Moreover, what exactly or even inexactly is the difference between claiming 'God is the universe and more' and 'God is the universe'? The trouble here, note, is not just vagueness – that is surely tolerable and indeed even expectable in religious discourse – but intelligibility. Thirdly, to so 'salvage' God-talk raises problems about what happens to the rather standard Christian claim that God is transcendent to the world. Presumably, the reply would be that 'the more' somehow gives something of the sense of 'transcendence' here. But to conceive of God as the universe viewed in a certain way and something more as well is a considerable reduction from the traditional claim that God is the very creator of the universe upon whom the universe depends while God depends on nothing Himself. Yet with this reductionist account we *may* get something somewhat more

97

coherent and less in conflict with our secular and scientific culture.[15] But, as MacIntyre is fond of pointing out, we have, if we take this turning, radically impoverished our religious claims by so de-mythologising them.[16] (However, apropos my second point, I would still like to insist that the de-mythologising is very incomplete.) Fourthly, the above theological talk about the universe as a basis for a single individuation for 'God', giving 'God' an identifying reference, mistakenly and incoherently reifies 'the universe'. As Russell and others have shown, no sense has been given to treating the universe as an entity, a thing or a class. Such talk about the universe is just plain mystifying reification.

There are, however, some further and even more fundamental things that I would like to say.

(1) According to the above objection, I presumably do a conjuring trick with 'God'. First I treat 'God' as a word which does not stand for any determinate, discrete reality in order to show that there is a problem about the reference of 'God', and then I insist on the propriety of asking *what* is this God, thereby inconsistently treating 'God' as if it were to be thought of as a term standing for a determinate discrete reality. However, it is not I who treat 'God' this way, but it is the very use of 'God' which has this incoherence in it. On the one hand, God is not an object among objects and is not something whose essence, whose 'whatness', we can understand, but on the other hand, 'God' is presumably an expression used referringly and an expression used in sentences employed to make statements. But then it must be possible to say, at least in some stammering way, what God is so that we can ascertain the truth-value of the statements in question; but if we say *what* God is, we treat God as an object while it remains the case that it is a conceptual or grammatical remark to say God is not an object, a being among beings. The cleft and incoherence is in the very first-order God-talk itself and not in my metatheology – if one can so 'dignify' it with such a label.

(2) Whether one treats existence claims as a sub-class of experientially confirmable claims or not, presumably to make an existence claim is to make a true or false statement but if we do that, then surely we should, experientially or otherwise, be able to give some sort of indication of what it would be like for our claim to be true or false. If an utterance has truth-value,

98

we ought to be able, at least under optimum conditions, to say what its truth-value is. But with these non-anthropomorphic religious utterances this is just what we cannot do.

(3) Whether 'God' is taught extra-linguistically or intra-linguistically via descriptions, it is still crucial that we are able to indicate what we are talking about and as we have seen in Chapter Three, a *via negativia* will not do here. To say God is utterly unique or to say 'God is ultimate reality' is to say something with nil or at least nearly nil communication value. It merely covers over what is in reality a scepticism with consoling and mystifying phrases. If it really is absurd to speak of carrying out some kind of investigation to find out what God is, then this very truth attests to the fact that God-talk cannot sensibly be taken at face value, for if there is some kind of conceptual ban on finding out what God is, if the very idea is (as it seems to be) a kind of absurdity, then it can hardly be the case that 'God' is really being used as a term which is about some difficult to characterise but still objective reality. We have in effect Kierkegaard's subjective Christianity of commitment.[17] Christianity is now simply a way of life *cum* ceremony. It is no longer as well a set of cosmological truth-claims.

Generally the central matter at issue here in these arguments and counter-arguments between sceptics and believers is that once we leave the absurdly false but intelligible claims of a very anthropomorphic and religiously and rationally unacceptable theism, we get versions of Christianity and Judaism which make central claims which are indeed alleged truth-claims but for them it cannot be ascertained under what conditions they would be true or probably true and under what conditions they would be false or probably false, and thus, their logical status and indeed their very intelligibility and coherence is problematical or anomalous.[18] This is readily explained if we accept some weak kind of verificationism, but whether or not we accept it, we still have the difficult and scepticism-supporting fact that we have here, at the very heart of these religions, key utterances supposedly making truth-claims yet claims concerning whose truth or falsity we remain utterly at sea. That is to say, we are at sea about them as we are at sea about 'It is five p.m. on Neptune'. The language is familiar but 'the truth' is not.

There is a moral dimension to this. Many people hang on to religion and stress the necessity of a religious orientation, for they feel that with the loss of religious belief there will be a moral decay or at least a sense of a loss of orientation and purpose. Life, under such circumstances, can have no *overall* rationale or purpose. In the West at least, secular *Weltanschauungen* have not taken up the slack for significantly large numbers of people. People are increasingly secularised without having a secularist world view.[19] But for people who remain or become genuinely religious their religion has this orienting function. For people who think they can make sense of the concept of God and retain their Jewish or Christian orientations, Father Copleston is surely correct in remarking that:

God is much more than an explanation, even an ultimate explanation. For profound religious faith God is *alpha* and *omega*, the beginning and the end. He is the ever-present reality in which (or, rather, in whom) we live and move and have our being, and whose creative activity is at work every where and at all times. For the real believer, God is the key-concept in a total vision of the world and of human life and history, a vision which forms the framework of the believer's life and which influences his outlook on himself and other men, his conduct, his hopes and his ideals.[20]

Moreover, while it is perfectly true that there are sceptics who have and do give sense to their lives and have a profoundly moral orientation and while it is also true that devout Catholics were among the guards of Nazi concentration camps and pious Protestants engaged in the wanton bombing of Dresden and Hiroshima, it remains the case that for many human beings their sense of moral orientation is closely linked with their religious commitments. That the connection is contingent has been demonstrated by arguments which go back to Plato's *Euthyphro*. It is not the case that we can identify what we ought to do with divine commands and it is the case that to understand what, if anything, could count as a being *worthy* of worship presupposes that we have some logically prior understanding of morality and what would constitute a justified moral claim.

Religion is in this important way dependent on morality, not morality on religion.[21]

Even when this is rightly understood and accepted, it remains true, as John MacQuarrie has argued, that unlike the secularist the Christian can pursue the demands that morality makes on him with the hope and trust that since God exists somehow good will ultimately prevail. If his beliefs make sense and are not evacuated of all their substance by contemporary demythologising, the religious man can believe in such an ultimate triumph of the Good in a way that is difficult, though perhaps not impossible, for the sceptic to believe in or perhaps even to make sense of.

Surely there is that difference and it is an important one – a difference that might lead a morally reflective man to probe with the greatest care the logic of religious belief to try to make as certain as he could whether there was a core of sense to religious claims. It indeed might lead such a man to retain or adopt a fideistic religious commitment even while acknowledging that the sceptic's case *seems* overwhelmingly strong. And there would be nothing irrational in that if indeed religious claims do make sense.

However, it is the case, as MacIntyre has stressed, that there comes a time when all the intellectual difficulties, scientific and philosophical, the moral perplexities about religion, the profoundly secular thrust of our culture and its altered conception of morality, taken together, make the whole Jewish or Christian world view no longer a live option in spite of its moral attractiveness in holding out a hope for some final triumph of the good.[22] Surely there are many people who are not there yet, but more and more are on their way or are in some state approximating this. What we need to realise is that the core ways of understanding ourselves and the world, the ways of living and indeed the very sensibilities of contemporary life are so thoroughly antithetical to the kinds of cosmological conceptions that could give those moral hopes sense that our culture's moral orientation, including the moral orientation of its most sensitive and reflective members, simply drifts away from such religious moral hopes and orientations. And at this point there remains to be accomplished a human and moral coming to terms with a new or a radically altered morla outlook, a tack that Nietzsche, Feuerbach and Marx realised was such a profound human and social problem. It is not the problem of finding a secular framework for the old religiously embedded moral beliefs but the problem of articulating, taking to heart and coming to live with, a profoundly altered conception of man's nature and destiny.

Wittgensteinian Fideists (e. g. D. Z. Phillips) would have it that what such considerations show is *not* the inadequacy of Christianity but 'the latent inadequacy of philosophical *theories* about religious beliefs . . .'[23] Such Fideists claim that philosophical critics of religion are in the grip of these mistaken philosophical accounts and, being in their grip, they suffer a decline of religious sensibility. What we must come to see, they claim, is that in 'so far as people believe in God, they do not believe in theories; but admittedly, theories about religion often make it difficult to believe in God'.[24]

It was the intent of Chapter Two to exhibit the inadequacy of such fideistic responses.[25] What Phillips calls a decline of religious sensibility, and what I would prefer to call a growing conviction that religion just does not make sense, often develops quite independently of any philosophical account. Someone afflicted with what Phillips calls positivism gives a certain, rather more precise articulation to what he already feels. That is, he gives one of several available rationales for his pervasive scepticism about religious belief. But the doubts were already there independently of positivism and the question of how these alleged truth-claims could indeed be true is not the creature of his newly acquired positivist or quasi-positivist philosophical beliefs, though he will have found a new and perhaps more adequate way of articulating them. But such doubt is not just the creature of a philosophical fashion. Moreover, the very accounts of Christian discourse given by Wittgensteinian Fideists do not help save a sceptic, for they leave us utterly in the dark as to how we could know or even coherently believe that these Christian claims are true. Being in the dark in this way may indeed be the first stage in the developnemt of a new sensibility, namely the cultural victory of scepticism. Beyond this there is the task of articulating a new outlook on man and the world. A task recognised and accepted by Nietzsche, Feuerbach and Marx and, their efforts not withstanding, a task yet to be completed.

102

Notes and References

Chapter 1

1. Peter Unger, 'A Defense of Skepticism', *The Philosophical Review*, vol. LXXX, no. 2 (April 1971) pp. 198–219. Note also Keith Lehrer, 'Why Not Scepticism?', *The Philosophical Forum* (1971).
2. Peter Unger, *The Philosophical Review*, p. 198.
3. Some of the doubts that beset people are well characterised by Frederick Copleston, 'The Special Features of Contemporary Atheism', *Twentieth Century: An Australian Quarterly Review*, vol. 25 (Spring 1970) pp. 5–15; Norwood Russell Hanson, 'What I Don't Believe', *Continuum*, vol. v, no. 1 (Spring 1967) pp. 89–105; and Ronald Hepburn, *Christianity and Paradox* (New York, Humanities Press, 1958).
4. Ninian Smart, *Philosophers and Religious Truth* (New York, The Macmillan Company, 1970) p. 3.
5. William Alston, 'Unconscious Intellectual Dishonesty in Religion', in A. J. Bellinzoni, Jr. and T. V. Litzenburg, Jr. (eds.), *Intellectual Honesty and Religious Commitment* (Philadelphia, Fortress Press, 1969) p. 28.
6. Ninian Smart, *Philosophers and Religious Truth*, p. 9.
7. I have clarified this, argued extensively for it and considered a range of plausible counter-arguments in my 'Can Faith Validate God-Talk', Martin E. Marty and Dean G. Peerman (eds.), *New Theology*, no. 1 (New York, The Macmillan Company, 1964) pp. 131–49 and in my 'Religious Perplexity and Faith', *The Crane Review*, vol. VIII, no. 1 (Fall 1965) pp. 1–17.
8. See here John King-Farlow, *Reason and Religion* (London, Darton, Longman & Todd Ltd., 1969) Chapter One and his 'Justifications of Religious Belief', *Philosophical Quarterly*, vol. XII, no. 3 (Fall 1962) pp. 261–3.
9. Hugo Meynell, 'Discussion of Language and the Concept

103

of God', *Question*, no. 5 (January 1972); *Sense and Nonsense and Christianity* (London, Sheed & Ward, 1964); and *The New Theology and Modern Theologians* (London, Sheed & Ward, 1967). John Wilson, *Philosophy and Religion: The Logic of Religious Belief* (London, Oxford University Press, 1961). I have critically examined Wilson's views in my '"Christian Positivism" and the Appeal to Religious Experience', *Journal of Religion*, vol. 42 (1962).

10. See Hugo Meynell's specification of what he takes to be the core of reductionist analyses in his *Sense and Nonsense and Christianity*, pp. 60–1.

11. Ninian Smart, 'The Intellectual Crisis of British Christianity', *New Theology*, no. 3 (New York, The Macmillan Company, 1966); 'Theology, Philosophy and the Natural Sciences', *An Inaugural Lecture*, University of Birmingham, March 1962 (Birmingham, The Kynock Press, 1962). F. C. Copleston, 'Man, Transcendence and the Absence of God', *Thought*, vol. XLIII (1968) pp. 24–38 and his reviews of Axel Hägerström's *Philosophy and Religion* and Richard Robinson's *An Atheist's Values* in the *Heythrop Journal*, vol. 7 (1966) and vol. 5 (1964) respectively.

12. See here Terence Penelhum, *Survival and Disembodied Existence* (London, Routledge & Kegan Paul, 1970) and Peter Geach, *God and the Soul* (London, Routledge & Kegan Paul, 1969) Chapters 1 and 2.

13. See John Hick, *Faith and Knowledge*, second edition (Ithaca, New York, Cornell University Press, 1966) pp. 189–99. I have criticised Hick's views on this matter in my 'Eschatological Verification' in Steven Cahn (ed.), *Philosophy of Religion* (New York, Harper & Row, 1970) and in my *Contemporary Critiques of Religion* (London, The Macmillan Press Ltd., 1971) pp. 71–93.

14. T. R. Miles, 'On Excluding the Supernatural', *Religious Studies*, vol. I, no. 2 (April 1966) and *Religion and the Scientific Outlook* (London, George Allen & Unwin Ltd., 1959).

15. Marcia Cavell, ' "God" and "The Self"', *The Journal of Religion*, forthcoming.

16. Paul Edwards, 'Kierkegaard and the "Truth" of Christianity', *Philosophy*, vol. XLVI (April 1971).

17. Ninian Smart, *The Philosophy of Religion* (New York, Random House, 1970).

18. Peter Slater, 'Current Trends in Analytic Philosophy of Religion', *Anviksiki*, vol. I, nos. 1 and 2 (August and December 1968) pp. 155–6.

19. This point has been argued in detail by I. T. Ramsey. See his *Religious Language* (London, SCM Press Ltd., 1957) and see Donald Evans' perceptive and systematic account of his theology. Donald Evans, 'Ian Ramsey on Talk About God', *Religious Studies*, vol. 7 (1971) pp. 125–40 and 213–26.

20. Marcia Cavell, 'Visions of a New Religion', *Saturday Review of Literature* (December 19, 1970) p. 13.

Chapter 2

1. See Paul L. Holmer, 'Wittgenstein and Theology', in Dallas M. High (ed.), *New Essays on Religious Language* (New York, Oxford University Press, 1969); 'Atheism and Theism', *Lutheran World*, vol. XII (1963); and 'Metaphysics and Theology: The Foundations of Theology', *The Lutheran Quarterly* (1967). See D. Z. Phillips, *The Concept of Prayer* (London, Routledge & Kegan Paul, 1965); *Faith and Philosophical Enquiry* (London, Routledge & Kegan Paul, 1970); *Death and Immortality* (London, Macmillan, 1970); the essays by Phillips in the volume he edited, D. Z. Phillips (ed.), *Religion and Understanding* (Oxford, Basil Blackwell, 1967), 'Religion and Epistemology: Some Contemporary Confusions', *Australasian Journal of Philosophy* (1966); and 'Religious Belief and Philosophical Enquiry', *Theology*, vol. LXXI, no. 573 (March 1968).

2. Phillips, *Faith and Philosophical Enquiry*, p. 166.

3. Ibid., p. 113.

4. Ibid., p. 157.

5. Ibid.

6. Ibid., p. 87.

7. Ibid., p. 89.

8. Ibid., p. 101.

9. Holmer, *The Lutheran World*, p. 15.

10. Ibid., p. 20.

11. Phillips, *Religion and Understanding*, p. 6.

12. Ibid., p. 68.

13. Ibid., p. 70.

14. Ibid., p. 71.

15. Phillips, *Religion and Understanding*, p. 73.
16. Ibid., p. 73.
17. Ibid., p. 75.
18. Søren Kierkegaard, *The Works of Love* (New York, Harper & Row, 1962) p. 42.
19. Phillips, *Theology*, pp. 120–1.
20. Ibid., p. 115.
21. Kai Nielsen, 'Wittgensteinian Fideism', *Philosophy* (July 1967).
22. Phillips, *Faith and Philosophical Enquiry*, p. 111.
23. Ibid., p. 117.
24. Ibid.
25. W. D. Hudson, 'Some Remarks on Wittgenstein's Account of Religious Belief', in *Talk of God*, Royal Institute of Philosophy Lectures vol. 2 (London, Macmillan, 1969) p. 44.
26. Basil Mitchell, 'The Justification of Religious Belief', *Philosophical Quarterly*, vol. ii (1961), reprinted in High (ed.), *New Essays on Religious Language*.
27. Robert C. Coburn, 'A Budget of Theological Puzzles', *Journal of Religion*, vol. xliii (April 1963) pp. 89–90.

Chapter 3

1. George I. Mavrodes, *Belief in God* (New York, Random House, 1970).
2. Ibid., p. 62.
3. Ibid., p. 50.
4. Ibid., p. 51.
5. Ibid., p. 62.
6. Ibid., p. 67.
7. Ibid., p. 63.
8. Ibid., p. 67.
9. Ibid., p. 68.
10. Ibid., p. 69.
11. Ibid.
12. Ibid.
13. Ibid., pp. 79, 86–7.
14. Ibid., p. 87.
15. See here particularly Frederick Copleston, *Thought*, pp. 33–4.

16. Mavrodes, *Belief in God*, p. 86.

17. Ibid., p. 79.

18. This criticism was made of my 'In Defense of Atheism', Howard E. Kiefer and Milton K. Munitz (eds.), *Perspectives in Education, Religion and the Arts* (Albany, New York, State University of New York Press, 1970) by John MacQuarrie in his 'Philosophy of Religion: A Response' in the same volume. The remainder of Section II of the present Chapter in effect constitutes my reply.

19. I. T. Ramsey, *Religious Language* and 'Talking About God' in I. T. Ramsey (ed.), *Words About God* (London, S.C.M. Press, 1971). Donald Evans, *Religious Studies*, pp. 125–40 and 213–26; 'Differences Between Scientific and Religious Assertions', in Ian G. Barbour (ed.), *Science and Religion* (New York, Harper & Row, 1968), pp. 101–33; and 'Barth on Talk About God', *Canadian Journal of Theology*, vol. XVI, nos. 3 and 4 (1970) pp. 175–92.

20. I. T. Ramsey, 'Introduction' to *Words About God*, pp. 12–13.

21. Athanasius, *Contr. Gent.*, 2. 35.

22. Origen, *De Prin.*, 1.

23. Basil, *Adv. Eun.*, 1. 2.

24. Gregory Nazianzen, *Orat.*, 34.

25. Hilary of Poictiers, *De Trin.*, 1. 19.

26. Ronald Hepburn, 'Agnosticism', Paul Edwards (ed.), *Encyclopedia of Philosophy*, vol. I (New York, Macmillan, 1967) p. 58.

27. Thomas S. Kuhn, *The Structure of Scientific Revolutions* (Chicago, University of Chicago Press, 1962). See also Paul K. Feyerabend, 'The Mind–Body Problem', *Continuum*, vol. V, no. 1 (Spring 1967) pp. 35–49.

28. Alastair McKinnon, *Falsification and Belief* (The Hague, Mouton & Co., 1970) p. 60.

29. Central arguments against such a conception of private language are developed in Ludwig Wittgenstein, *Philosophical Investigations*, G. E. M. Anscombe, trans. (Oxford, Basil Blackwell, 1953) and *The Blue and Brown Books* (Oxford, Basil Blackwell, 1958). See also Peter Winch, *The Idea of a Social Science* (London, Routledge & Kegan Paul, 1958) Chapter One. There is further literature on the subject in George Pitcher (ed.), *Wittgenstein: The Philosophical Investigations, A Collection of Critical Essays* (Garden City, New York, Doubleday & Com-

pany, Inc., 1966); Harold Morick (ed.), *Wittgenstein and the Problem of Other Minds* (Toronto, McGraw-Hill Book Company, 1967); John Turk Saunders and Donald F. Henze, *The Private-Language Problem* (New York, Random House, 1967); and Stanley Cavell, *Must We Mean What We Say* (New York, Charles Scribner's Sons, 1969) pp. 1–72 and pp. 238–66.

30. Ninian Smart, *The Philosophy of Religion* (Random House, New York, 1970) pp. 41–4.

31. T. R. Miles, 'On Excluding the Supernatural', *Religious Studies*, vol. 1, no. 2 (April 1966) p. 150.

Chapter 4

1. Donald Evans, *Science and Religion*; Donald Evans, *The Logic of Self-Involvement*, (New York, Herder & Herder, 1969); Ninian Smart, *Reasons and Faiths* (London, Routledge & Kegan Paul, 1958); Ninian Smart, *Philosophers and Religious Truth*; Ninian Smart, *An Inaugural Lecture*, University of Birmingham, 1962; Ninian Smart, *The Philosophy of Religion*; Ian Crombie, 'Theology and Falsification', in Antony Flew and Alasdair MacIntyre (eds.), *New Essays in Philosophical Theology*; Ian Crombie, 'The Possibility of Theological Statements' in Basil Mitchell (ed.), *Faith and Logic* (London, George Allen & Unwin, Ltd., 1957); Ian T. Ramsey, 'Talking About God' in Ian T. Ramsey (ed.), *Words About God*; Ian T. Ramsey, *Christian Discourse* (London, Oxford University Press, 1965); Ian T. Ramsey, *Religious Language* (London, S.C.M. Press, 1957); Ian T. Ramsey, 'On Understanding Mystery', *Chicago Theological Register*, vol. 53 (May 1963); Ian T. Ramsey, *Models and Mystery* (London, Oxford University Press, 1964). There is an excellent review article of Ramsey's work by Donald Evans in *Religious Studies*, vol. 7 (1971) pp. 125–40 and 213–26. Gordon D. Kaufman, 'On the Meaning of "God": Transcendence Without Mythology', *The Harvard Theological Review*, vol. 59, no. 2 (April 1966); Gordon D. Kaufman, 'On the Meaning of "Act of God"', *Harvard Theological Review*, vol. 61 (1968) pp. 175–201; and Gordon D. Kaufman, 'Two Models of Transcendence', in R. E. Cashman and E. Grislis, *The Heritage of Christian Thought* (New York, Harper & Row, 1965).

2. Ninian Smart, *The Philosophy of Religion*, p. 49.

3. Ibid., p. 51.
4. Ibid., p. 69.
5. Ibid., p. 59.
6. Ian Crombie, 'The Possibility of Theological Statements', in Basil Mitchell (ed.), *Faith and Logic* (Allen & Unwin, London, 1957) pp. 31–83.
7. Smart, op. cit., pp. 59–60.
8. In this context see Alice Ambrose, 'The Problem of Linguistic Inadequacy', in Max Black (ed.), *Philosophical Analysis* (Ithaca, New York, Cornell University Press, 1950) and William Kennick, 'Art and the Ineffable', *Journal of Philosophy*, vol. 58 (1961) pp. 309–20.
9. Smart, op. cit., p. 76.
10. Donald D. Evans, *Science and Religion*, p. 103.
11. Ibid., p. 104.
12. Ibid.
13. Ibid.
14. Ibid., p. 105.
15. Ibid., pp. 107–8.
16. Donald Evans, *The Logic of Self Involvement*, p. 128.
17. Ibid.
18. Ibid.
19. Ibid., p. 133.
20. Ibid.
21. Ibid., p. 134.
22. Ibid., p. 135.
23. Ibid.
24. Ibid.
25. Ibid., p. 251.
26. Ibid.
27. Donald Evans, *Science and Religion*, p. 109.
28. Ibid., pp. 127–8.
29. Remember that understanding admits of degrees. I am not saying that there could be no understanding of religion or even some minimal kind of adherence to a religion without these attitudes, but I do take it as a conceptual remark about Judaism and Christianity at least that without such attitudes there would be no full or even adequate understanding of such religions.
30. Donald Evans, *Science and Religion*, p. 127.
31. Ibid.

32. Donald Evans, *Science and Religion*, p. 109.

33. Ibid., p. 131.

34. Gordon Kaufman, *The Harvard Theological Review*, pp. 105–32.

35. Ibid., p. 106.

36. Father Copleston also shows an awareness of how central this problem is in our contemporary thinking about religion. See F. C. Copleston, *Thought*, pp. 24–38 and *Twentieth Century: An Australian Quarterly Review*, pp. 5–14.

37. Kaufman, *The Harvard Theological Review*, p. 109.

38. Ibid., p. 110.

39. Ibid.

40. Ibid., p. 112.

41. Ibid.

42. Ibid.

43. Ibid., p. 113.

44. Ibid.

45. Ibid., p. 114.

46. Ibid., p. 116.

47. Ibid., p. 115.

48. Ibid., p. 120.

49. Ibid., p. 121.

50. Ibid., pp. 126–9.

51. Ibid., p. 122.

52. Ibid., p. 124.

53. Ibid., pp. 125–6.

54. In addition to the present essay under discussion, see here as well Gordon Kaufman, 'Philosophy of Religion and Christian Theology', *The Journal of Religion* (October 1957). But see in response my 'The Primacy of Philosophical Theology', *Theology Today*, vol. xxvii, no. 2 (July 1970) pp. 155–69.

55. Gordon Kaufman, *The Harvard Theological Review*, p. 126.

56. Ibid.

57. Ibid.

58. Ibid., pp. 126–7.

59. Ibid., p. 128.

60. Gilbert Ryle, *The Concept of Mind* (London, Hutchinson's University Library, 1949); Ludwig Wittgenstein, *Philosophical Investigations*; Stuart Hampshire, *Thought and Action* (London, Chatto & Windus, 1959); Bernard Williams, 'Imagination and

the Self', *British Academy* (1966); Peter Strawson, *Individuals* (London, Methuen & Co. Ltd., 1959).

61. Gordon Kaufman, *The Harvard Theological Review*, p. 126.
62. Peter Strawson, *Individuals*.
63. I argue this in some detail in my *Contemporary Critiques of Religion* (London, Macmillan, 1971), Chapter 6.
64. Gordon Kaufman, *The Harvard Theological Review*, p. 129.
65. Ibid., compare pages 151 and 132.
66. Ibid., p. 123.
67. Ian T. Ramsey, 'Talking About God', in his *Words About God*, pp. 202–23.
68. Ibid., p. 211.
69. Ibid., p. 212.
70. Ibid., pp. 205–6.
71. Ibid., p. 212.
72. Ibid.
73. Ibid.
74. Ibid.
75. Ibid., p. 202.
76. Ibid., p. 211.
77. Ibid., p. 213.
78. Ibid.
79. Ibid., p. 214.
80. Ibid., p. 211.

Chapter 5

1. Norwood Russell Hanson, *Continuum*, pp. 89–105; Sidney Hook, *The Quest For Being* (New York, St Martin's Press, 1961); Wallace I. Matson, *The Existence of God* (Ithaca, New York, Cornell University Press, 1965); Ernest Nagel, 'Philosophical Concepts of Atheism' in Johnson E. Fairchild (ed.), *Basic Beliefs* (New York, Hart Publishing Company, Inc., 1959) pp. 173–92; Michael Scriven, *Primary Philosophy* (New York, McGraw-Hill Book Company, 1966) Chapter IV.
2. Hanson, *Continuum*, p. 93.
3. Paul K. Feyerabend, *Continuum*, pp. 35–49.
4. F. C. Copleston, *Heythrop Journal*, p. 405.
5. Alasdair MacIntyre, 'The Debate About God: Victorian Relevance and Contemporary Irrelevance' in Alasdair MacIntyre and Paul Ricoeur, *The Religious Significance of Atheism*

(New York, Columbia University Press, 1969) p. 19. See also on this point, Terence Penelhum, *Religion and Rationality* (New York, Random House, 1971) pp. 154–61.

6. See Sidney Hook, *The Quest for Being*, pp. 115–35 and 143–95. I have criticised this account and indicated where it is question-begging in my 'Religion and Naturalistic Humanism: Some Remarks on Hook's Critique of Religion' in Paul Kurtz (ed.), *Sidney Hook and the Contemporary World* (New York, The John Day Company, 1968) pp. 257–80.

7. One may be tempted to think this is not so because one may think 'there is no one reality which protects finite creatures' is plainly confirmable, though not, of course, decisively confirmable. Mothers protect their children, bears their cubs, hills facing the south protect the grapes and the like. But note that the man who tries to assert 'God protects his creation' does not deny such things but still he doesn't take them as counting against his religious claim either; and similarly the atheist who tries to assert 'There is no one transcendent reality which protects finite creatures' can't say what counts against the truth of his claim. It isn't that I am asking for *decisive* confirmation or disconfirmation here, but only for a specification of evidence that would enable us to distinguish these putative claims.

8. E. L. Mascall, *The Openness of Being* (London, Darton, Longman & Todd, 1971) p. 63.

9. Tziporah Kasachkoff, 'Talk About God's Existence', *Philosophical Studies* (The National University of Ireland) vol. XIX (1970) pp. 181–92.

10. Ibid., pp. 191–2.

11. Claims (2) and (3) are argued forcefully by Diogenes Allen, *The Reasonableness of Faith* (Washington-Cleveland, Corpus Books, 1968). But for difficulties in this account see my review in *Theology Today*, vol. XXVI, no. 3 (October 1969) pp. 344–6.

12. Rush Rhees, *Without Answers* (London, Routledge & Kegan Paul, 1969) p. 114.

13. Ibid., p. 127.

14. Donald Evans, *Religious Studies*, p. 135.

15. John MacQuarrie has argued in this way in trying to meet the falsification challenge in his 'On Gods and Gardeners'. I have tried to exhibit its utter lack of success in my response

112

'On Waste and Wastelands'. Both of these essays occur in Howard E. Kiefer and Milton K. Munitz (eds.), *Perspectives in Education, Religion and the Arts.*

16. Alasdair MacIntyre, *Against the Self-Images of the Age* (London, Gerald Duckworth & Company, Ltd., 1971) pp. 12–26. See also my 'Religion and Commitment', Robert H. Ayers and William T. Blackstone (eds.), *Religious Language and Knowledge* (Athens, Georgia, University of Georgia Press, 1972) pp. 18–43.

17. Paul Edwards, *Philosophy*, pp. 89–108.

18. I have argued this in some detail in my *Contemporary Critiques of Religion.*

19. See here Alasdair MacIntyre, *Marxism and Christianity* (London, Gerald Duckworth and Company, Ltd., 1969) Chapter One and *Secularization and Moral Change* (London, Oxford University Press, 1967).

20. F. C. Copleston, *Twentieth Century: An Australian Quarterly Review*, p. 8.

21. I have argued for this in Chapter Twenty-two of my *Reason and Practice* (New York, Harper and Row, 1971). I have further developed this argument in my *Ethics Without God* (London, Pemberton Publishing Co. Ltd., 1973). These issues are aired from several points of view in the essays reprinted by Ian T. Ramsey (ed.), *Christian Ethics and Contemporary Philosophy* (London, S.C.M. Press Ltd., 1966).

22. Alasdair MacIntyre, 'Is Understanding Religion Compatible with Believing?' in John Hick (ed.), *Faith and the Philosophers* (New York, St Martin's Press Inc., 1964) and in 'The Debate About God: Victorian Relevance and Contemporary Irrelevance' in *The Religious Significance of Atheism.*

23. D. Z. Phillips, 'Review of *The Religious Significance of Atheism*', *The Philosophical Quarterly*, vol. 21, no. 82 (January 1971) p. 93.

24. Ibid. See also Rush Rhees, *Without Answers*, pp. 110–32.

25. See also my *Contemporary Critiques of Religion*, Chapter 5.

Bibliography

Allen, Diogenes. *The Reasonableness of Faith.* Washington-Cleveland: Corpus Books, 1968.

Ayers, Robert H. and Blackstone, William T. (eds.). *Religious Language and Knowledge.* Athens, Georgia: University of Georgia Press, 1972.

Barbour, Ian G. (ed.). *Science and Religion.* New York: Harper & Row, 1968.

Bellinzoni, A. J., Jr. and Litzenburg, T. V., Jr. (eds.). *Intellectual Dishonesty and Religious Commitment.* Philadelphia: Fortress Press, 1969.

Black, Max (ed.). *Philosophical Analysis.* Ithaca, New York: Cornell University Press, 1950.

Cahn, Steven (ed.). *Philosophy of Religion.* New York: Harper & Row, 1970.

Cashman, R. E. and Grislis, E. *The Heritage of Christian Thought.* New York: Harper & Row, 1965.

Cavell, Stanley. *Must We Mean What We Say.* New York: Charles Scribner's Sons, 1969.

Edwards, Paul (ed.). *Encyclopedia of Philosophy.* New York: Macmillan, 1967.

Evans, Donald. *The Logic of Self-Involvement.* New York: Herder & Herder, 1969.

Fairchild, Johnson E. (ed.). *Basic Beliefs.* New York: Hart Publishing Co. Inc., 1959.

Flew, Antony and MacIntyre, Alasdair (eds.). *New Essays in Philosophical Theology.* New York: The Macmillan Company, 1955.

Geach, Peter. *God and the Soul.* London: Routledge & Kegan Paul, 1969.

Hampshire, Stuart. *Thought and Action.* London: Chatto & Windus, 1959.

Hepburn, Ronald. *Christianity and Paradox.* New York: Humanities Press, 1958.

115

Hick, John. *Faith and Knowledge*, second edition. Ithaca, New York: Cornell University Press, 1966.

Hick, John. *Faith and the Philosophers*. New York: St Martin's Press Inc., 1964.

High, Dallas M. (ed.). *New Essays on Religious Language*. New York: Oxford University Press, 1969.

Hook, Sidney. *The Quest for Being*. New York: St Martin's Press Inc., 1961.

Kiefer, Howard E. and Munitz, Milton K. (eds.). *Perspectives in Education, Religion and the Arts*. Albany, New York: State University of New York Press, 1970.

Kierkegaard, Søren. *The Works of Love*. New York: Harper & Row, 1962.

King-Farlow, John. *Reason and Religion*. London: Darton, Longman & Todd Ltd., 1969.

Kurtz, Paul (ed.). *Sidney Hook and the Contemporary World*. New York: The John Day Company, 1968.

Kuhn, Thomas S. *The Structure of Scientific Revolutions*. Chicago: University of Chicago Press, 1962.

MacIntyre, Alasdair. *Against the Self-Images of the Age*. London: Gerald Duckworth & Company, Ltd., 1971.

MacIntyre, Alasdair. *Marxism and Christianity*. London: Gerald Duckworth and Company, Ltd., 1969.

MacIntyre, Alasdair. *Secularization and Moral Change*. London: Oxford University Press, 1967.

MacIntyre, Alasdair and Ricoeur, Paul. *The Religious Significance of Atheism*. New York: Columbia University Press, 1969.

MacKinnon, Alastair. *Falsification and Belief*. The Hague: Mouton & Co., 1970.

Marty, Martin E. and Peerman, Dean G. (eds.). *New Theology*, no. 1. New York: The Macmillan Company, 1964.

Mascall, E. L. *The Openness of Being*. London: Darton, Longman & Todd Ltd., 1971.

Matson, Wallace I. *The Existence of God*. Ithaca, New York: Cornell University Press, 1965.

Mavrodes, George I. *Belief in God*. New York: Random House, 1970.

Meynell, Hugo. *Sense and Nonsense and Christianity*. London: Sheed and Ward, 1964.

Meynell, Hugo. *The New Theology and Modern Theologians* London: Sheed & Ward, 1967.
116

Miles, T. E. *Religion and the Scientific Outlook*. London: George Allen & Unwin Ltd., 1959.

Mitchell, Basil (ed.). *Faith and Logic*. London: George Allen & Unwin Ltd., 1957.

Morick, Harold (ed.). *Wittgenstein and the Problem of Other Minds*. Toronto: McGraw-Hill Book Company, 1967.

Nielsen, Kai. *Contemporary Critiques of Religion*. London: The Macmillan Press Ltd., 1971.

Nielsen, Kai. *Ethics Without God*. London: Pemberton Publishing Co. Ltd., 1973.

Nielsen, Kai. *Reason and Practice*. New York: Harper & Row, 1971.

Penelhum, Terence. *Survival and Disembodied Existence*. London: Routledge & Kegan Paul, 1970.

Phillips, D. Z. *The Concept of Prayer*. London: Routledge & Kegan Paul, 1965.

Phillips, D. Z. *Death and Immortality*. London: Macmillan, 1970.

Phillips, D. Z. *Faith and Philosophical Enquiry*. London: Routledge & Kegan Paul, 1970.

Phillips, D. Z. *Religion and Understanding*. Oxford: Basil Blackwell, 1967.

Pitcher, George (ed.). *Wittgenstein: The Philosophical Investigations A Collection of Critical Essays*. Garden City, New York: Doubleday & Company Inc., 1966.

Ramsey, Ian T. *Christian Discourse*. London: Oxford University Press, 1965.

Ramsey, Ian T. (ed.). *Christian Ethics and Contemporary Philosophy*. London: S.C.M. Press, 1966.

Ramsey, Ian T. *Models and Mystery*. London: Oxford University Press, 1964.

Ramsey, Ian T. *Religious Language*. London: S.C.M. Press, 1957.

Ramsey, Ian T. (ed.). *Words About God*. London: S.C.M. Press, 1971.

Rhees, Rush. *Without Answers*. London: Routledge & Kegan Paul, 1969.

Ryle, Gilbert. *The Concept of Mind*. London: Hutchinson's University Library, 1949.

Saunders, John Turk and Henze, Donald F. *The Private-Language Problem*. New York: Random House, 1967.

Scriven, Michael. *Primary Philosophy*. New York: McGraw-Hill Book Company, 1966.

117

Smart, Ninian. *Philosophers and Religious Truth*. New York: The Macmillan Company, 1970.

Smart, Ninian. *The Philosophy of Religion*. New York: Random House, 1970.

Smart, Ninian. *Reasons and Faiths*. London: Routledge & Kegan Paul, 1958.

Strawson, Peter. *Individuals*. London: Methuen & Co. Ltd., 1959.

Wilson, John. *Philosophy and Religion: The Logic of Religious Belief*. London: Oxford University Press, 1961.

Winch, Peter. *The Idea of a Social Science*. London: Routledge & Kegan Paul, 1958.

Wittgenstein, Ludwig. *The Blue and Brown Books*. Oxford: Basil Blackwell, 1958.

Wittgenstein, Ludwig. *Philosophical Investigations*, translated by G. E. M. Anscombe. Oxford: Basil Blackwell, 1953.